THE LOGIC OF
DETERRENCE

THE LOGIC OF DETERRENCE

Anthony Kenny

Firethorn Press

First published in Great Britain in 1985 by
Waterstone & Co Limited
193 Kensington High Street
London W8 6SH

Firethorn Press is an imprint of
Waterstone & Co Limited

ISBN 0-947752-07-2

Typeset by Concept Communications, Dartford, Kent.

Printed and bound by Whitstable Litho Ltd,
Whitstable, Kent.

Distributed by Sidgwick & Jackson Limited
1 Tavistock Chambers
Bloomsbury Way
London WC1A 2SG

CONTENTS

PREFACE

This book is the result of reflection on the logic and ethics of nuclear deterrence which has continued for more than 20 years. It was Professor G.E.M. Anscombe who first caused me to be seriously concerned about the topic, and this book owes a lot to her pamphlet *Mr Truman's Degree* and her later written and oral discussions. My first publication on this issue was "Counterforce and Countervalue", a discussion of Mr McNamara's Ann Arbor speech of 1962, which appeared in the Catholic periodical *The Clergy Review* later in that year, and has been reprinted several times since. More recently, I contributed a paper "Better Dead than Red" to an anthology *Objections to Deterrence*, edited by Nigel Blake and Kay Pole (Routledge, 1984). Some of the material from that paper is used in the present work.

The main lines of this book derive from a seminar which I gave in Oxford in Hilary Term 1984 with Mr David Fisher of the Ministry of Defence. I learnt much from Mr Fisher and from the participants in that class, and I wish to thank him and them. Two of the papers delivered to that class have been published, in their original version, in a collection of my papers entitled *Philosophy and Polity* (Blackwell, 1985).

I am much indebted to Stan Windass, Frank Barnaby, Sir Hugh Beach and other members of the *Just Defence* group for their careful exploration of realistic alternatives to our present defence policies. But for all my debts to others, the views expressed here are, of course, entirely my own responsibility.

INTRODUCTION

Nuclear war, nuclear deterrence and nuclear disarmament are the three most important issues of public policy at the present time. Almost everyone holds nuclear war in horror. President Reagan, who has sometimes seemed to his critics the most bellicose of recent American leaders, has nonetheless gone on record as saying that a nuclear war cannot be won and must not be fought. Almost everyone, again, is in favour of nuclear disarmament: those who wish to preserve a massive nuclear arsenal describe themselves as "multilateral disarmers", and an increase in the nuclear armoury, such as the deployment of Cruise and Pershing-2 missiles, is described as a step towards a real reduction in nuclear arms. There is no reason to question the genuineness of our leaders' horror of nuclear war, or their desire for some form of nuclear disarmament, but it is by examining a person's attitude to nuclear deterrence that one can see the real significance of his or her stance towards war and disarmament.

Deterrence is the key concept for the understanding of the strategy and diplomacy of the age. It is the concept which is used to justify decisions of high cost and great moment. Deterrence is a simple idea, but like many simple ideas it has a complicated logic. This book will attempt to set out the logic of nuclear deterrence in such a way as to enable the reader to make a judgment on the rationality and morality of the policies which he or she is invoked to support. For only by understanding what is involved in deterrence can one apply the traditional ethics of war to the moral issues raised by nuclear weapons.

The book will fall into three parts. The first, **The Ethics of War**, will discuss whether the actual fighting of a nuclear war could be rational or morally acceptable, and I shall conclude that it could not. The second, **The Logic of Deterrence**, will inquire whether, notwithstanding this, it may be right and reasonable to pursue a policy of nuclear deterrence which has as its goal the prevention of nuclear war. I shall argue that the existing deterrent policies of both East and West are unacceptable on three grounds: that they are murderous, dangerous and extravagant. The third part, **The Realities of Disarmament**, will ask what policies, in the concrete, should be pursued by a society that resolves to forego reliance on the murderous threat implicit in our present strategies. I shall argue that there is room for real and prudent nuclear disarmament between the illusory hopes of the multilateralists who seek disarmament by negotiation and the impractical idealism of those who call for immediate and total unilateral disarmament by the West.

I. THE ETHICS OF WAR

1 Nuclear War
and Nuclear Catastrophe

Everyone knows that it is a terrible thing to be the victim of a nuclear attack. When the first atom bomb was dropped on Hiroshima at the end of the Second World War, more than half of the quarter of a million people who lived within three miles of the explosion were killed or injured. The bomb dropped on Hiroshima was a 12.5 kiloton bomb, that is to say it had an explosive power equivalent to that of 12,500 tons of TNT. Many contemporary weapons are far more powerful. Soviet SS-18 missiles, which have a range of 7,500 miles, carry 10 independently targetable warheads each with a payload of 750 kilotons. Hence they each incarnate as much explosive power as 60 Hiroshimas: 7.5 megatons or 7,500 kilotons. The Soviet Union has at its disposal 300 or more of these missiles, besides many of other kinds. The megatonnage of its strategic weapons alone is believed to be well in excess of 4,000mt. That is to say, it is equivalent to 320,000 Hiroshimas. If all this explosive power could be used in the way the atom bomb was over Hiroshima, there would be enough to kill about 22,000m people. But of course it could not: the world's population is not huddled together as people in the middle of Hiroshima. Moreover, there are only about 4,000m people in the world.

In a large-scale attack on the United States, however, it would be open to the Russians to fire 2,000 warheads at American cities, in addition to those aimed at military targets. This would allow 20 warheads for each of the six cities with a population of over a million, 10 warheads for each of the next

1

100 largest cities, and leave enough for one warhead for each town with more than a few thousand population. It has been surmised that in an all-out attack the 200 largest American cities would be obliterated within half an hour, and after an attack on this scale only 2% of the American urban population would survive.

A much smaller attack would suffice to wipe out a similar proportion of the smaller and more densely packed population of the United Kingdom. Prior to the deployment of cruise missiles in Britain, a number of studies estimated the likely scale of a wartime attack at around 200 megatons. Estimates of the deaths resulting from such an attack have varied, in accordance with different assumptions about targeting and other factors, from 20m to 34m, out of a total population in Great Britain of some 54m.

There are several different ways of dying from a nuclear attack. The fireball which develops around an exploding weapon will melt or evaporate everything and everybody within or around it. The heat radiated from the fireball will cause burns which may be lethal within one mile of a 20kt bomb: clothes may catch fire within two kilometres of the point beneath the explosion. A blast wave will demolish buildings and crush men beneath the debris, or sweep people up and crash them into the rubble. Up to a distance of two miles, most buildings will collapse. Meanwhile, lethal ionising radiation is emitted which will kill any survivor within a mile and a half of the explosion. Besides the direct radiation there will be fall-out radiation from material swept up and radioactivated by the explosion. People 100 miles downwind of the explosion may receive a lethal dose from this fall-out. No medical care could be expected by the fraction of the population that survived, and the great majority would be likely to die of famine and disease in the aftermath of the war. Scientists studying the global effects of nuclear war have estimated that a large-scale exchange (above 5,000mt, but well within the capacity of the combined world arsenal of over 12,000mt) would kill outright, by blast, heat and radiation, about 1,000m people. About the same number would be serious-ly injured, and would be likely to die for want of medical attention. That would mean that up to half the entire human race could be immediate victims of a nuclear war.

Nuclear Winter

Recent studies of the long-term effects of nuclear war suggest that those who survived the immediate conflict would not find it easy to keep themselves alive. After such a nuclear exchange, with 20% of the explosive power discharged on urban/industrial targets in the northern hemisphere, it has been predicted that an unbroken pall of darkness would cover the hemisphere, which might spread to the whole planet. This nuclear winter would affect victim and aggressor alike. The lack of sunlight would limit or halt plant growth and create a grave danger of famine. Temperatures would drop to freezing levels for several months, fresh water supplies would be frozen and most farm animals would die, causing many human survivors to starve. Radioactive fall-out over weeks, toxic gases released into the atmosphere from burning cities and ultra-violet radiation penetrating the damaged ozone shield would combine to cause organic damage and increase the probabilities of disease. Even relatively small exchanges could produce dramatic climatic changes: 100mt exploded in the air over cities could produce long periods of darkness and severe frost.

There was some initial scepticism about the predictions of a nuclear winter, first made by a small private group of scientists in the United States. But similar results were obtained by researchers in Great Britain and the Soviet Union. Finally the Pentagon asked the American National Academy of Sciences to study the evidence for the theory. The team of specialists pub-lished their report at the end of 1984. Their results largely confirmed the earlier findings. A nuclear exchange against the principal military targets and the 1,000 largest cities in the Nato and Warsaw Pact countries, using only half the stockpile of each of the superpowers, could pollute the atmosphere with dust and smoke for 6 to 20 weeks. If the war was waged in spring or summer, the resulting loss of sunlight could reduce temperatures in the northern hemisphere by between 18° and 55°. The freeze might last for months, with an almost total loss of light. Only those living in the southern hemisphere could hope to escape the worst of the war's impact.

There are now many books easily available which describe, in sober scientific detail, the magnitude of the nuclear catastrophe. The most authoritative, so far as concerns the United Kingdom, is the report of the British Medical Association's Board of Science and Education, *The Medical Effects of Nuclear War,* from which much of the information in the previous paragraphs has been taken. That report does not draw any conclusions about the politics of nuclear armament or disarmament: it restricts itself to an account of the medical consequences of the explosion of nuclear weapons.

This book is not intended to be one more dramatisation of the horrors of nuclear war. Nor will it attempt to excite in the reader fear and disgust of nuclear weapons, wholly appropriate though those emotions are at the prospect of their likely use. Its aim is to assist the reader to think clearly about an issue whose magnitude makes clear thought imperative, and whose horror makes it extraordinarily difficult.

The attempt to achieve rational judgment about the use and possession of nuclear weapons must begin with reflection on the nature and ethics of warfare. It is not enough, when faced with a portrayal of the intolerable outcome of a nuclear battle, to say that it is something which must be avoided at all costs and to cast about for the best way of ensuring that it does not happen. It is natural and correct to say that nuclear war is something to be avoided at all costs. But to base one's policies on that one premise in isolation may betray a misconception of the nature of war which risks bringing the ultimate disaster closer.

The most important thing about war is often forgotten because it is so obvious. War is a human creation: it is not a natural phenomenon like the eruption of a volcano or the outbreak of a plague. Waging war is a human activity, and like other human activities it is an object of rational deliberation and moral evaluation. War is the organised pursuit of political goals by the disciplined use of lethal force. Weapons of war are human tools whose use is to inflict death and injury upon those against whom one is warring, or to reduce one's enemies' capacity for inflicting death and injury upon one's own side. Nuclear weapons and all the hardware and software that constitute and support them are, like other weapons of war, human tools and instruments.

Because it is often forgotten that war is a human activity, something which is waged by human beings against each other, nuclear war comes to be thought of as simply an unmitigated disaster which must be guarded against as one would guard against a forest fire or an epidemic. However a nuclear war is not something which would happen to us: it is something in which we would take part. We need to consider in what circumstances, if any, it would be appropriate, rational or morally acceptable for us to take part in it. A one-sided nuclear attack, of course, is something that could happen to a country without any participation of its own. Self-interest, perhaps, might dictate that one's actions should be guided by the maxim: "Do whatever makes it most unlikely that one will be the victim of a nuclear attack." But any moral as distinct from merely prudential judgment would also have to take into account the interests of others, including the potential launchers of the attack upon one's own side. It may be that self-interest would decide that the surest way to ensure that one's own side was not the victim of a nuclear attack was to obliterate a hostile nation by a pre-emptive strike. But that would hardly settle the moral issue. It is not enough, when contemplating the scenario of a nuclear apocalypse, simply to say: "That must never happen."

The Error of Pacifism

Because war involves the deliberate killing of one's enemies, some have concluded that war is never justified. Respect for

5

human life, they argue, so overrides all other values that no political objective can justify the taking of life involved in war. Pacifism of this kind has always been the conviction of a minority. If it attracts more adherents at the present time than ever before, that is principally because many people believe that any future war will be, or will become, a nuclear war. Many people too, who are not opposed to war in principle, and who regard wars in the past as having been justified, are called and will call themselves "nuclear pacifists", because they believe that it can never be justified to fight a war with nuclear weapons. The expression is perhaps an unfortunate one, as if one were to call "gas pacifists" those who object to the use of chemical weapons in warfare. But it is too late to object to its employment, which need not be misleading so long as it is realised that a nuclear pacifist need not be a pacifist in the strict sense at all.

I believe that strict pacifism is mistaken, and that the fighting of wars can be and has been justified. Moreover, I think that what is wrong with pacifism is often mis-stated even by those who are themselves not pacifists. It is not that pacifism holds up a noble ideal which most human beings are too sinful to live up to. A pacifist administration may fail to protect the liberties of its subjects, and a pacifist citizen may fail to perform his allotted task in a just war. In both cases, these are not idealists performing a work of supererogation: however good their intentions, they are neglecting an important duty. Pacifism is a moral error no matter how noble the respect for life and love of peace which inspire it.

The pacifist's error with respect to nuclear war is at the opposite extreme to the mistake of treating it as a kind of natural catastrophe. War, even nuclear war, is not something which escapes the bounds of human responsibility, and yet war is not something which can never be responsibly embarked upon. A pacifist rules out nuclear war because he regards all war as an activity unworthy of human beings. It takes no dialectical skill to argue that if all war is wrong, then nuclear war is wrong. The more difficult and more pressing question, for those who are ready to accept war as a legitimate human institution, is whether nuclear weapons are a tolerable part of that institution in the twentieth century, and that in turn depends on the conditions under which war is lawfully waged. To a pacifist, consideration of the laws of war is otiose: at best it can have a sociological interest, like an investigation of what conduct is regarded as tolerable and what is intolerable within the confines of a Mafia family. But those who regard war as justified and sometimes necessary in an imperfect world must make clear to themselves and others what they regard as the conditions under which war can be waged, and the limits which are to be observed in its waging.

2 The Just War in the Nuclear Age

In rejecting pacifism I am claiming that there can be such a thing as a just war. It is possible, that is to say, to have a right to go to war, and to wage war morally, provided that certain conditions are fulfilled. We honour and ennoble soldiers and servicemen, and we are right to do so, if they have fought justly in a just war. Moreover, though many wars have been fought for bad causes, and many wars for good causes have been disfigured by crimes against the laws of war, the possibility of a just war is not a matter of idle theory. The defence of the independence of the nations of the West against aggression from the communist bloc, for instance, would in itself provide a just cause of war. Leaving aside for the moment the nuclear issue, it would be right to risk our own lives, and to take those of enemy combatants, to preserve our independence and our traditions.

A just war is not the same as a war in which both sides are acting justly. On most traditional definitions of a just war such a war is hard to conceive. If a war is to be just at all it must be waged in order to right a wrong done or prevent an imminent injustice. There cannot, therefore, be a war which is just in the sense that both the combatants are fully justified in fighting. However, given the complications of international relations, it may well be that both sides to a conflict may reasonably believe that they have a just cause. But even if it is the case that in most wars at least one side is acting unjustly, that does not render all war-making unjust: it can be just to make war in defence against those who are making war unjustly.

8

If it is dangerous to think of war as an impersonal event, as something which happens or breaks out, it is no less dangerous to think of it as a self-contained human activity like baseball or cricket or other games. To be justified, war must be an instrument of policy: it must be a means to a desirable and morally defensible goal. Victory is not in itself a goal which justifies war: to justify a war one must be able to point to the good to be achieved by victory. Winning a war is not like winning a game in which the aim is something defined by the internal structure of the activity. This means that the unconditional surrender of the enemy is not a legitimate objective of war: the justified purpose of the war itself sets the conditions under which surrender should be acceptable. Of course, it may be reasonable to adopt a policy of unconditional refusal to deal with a particular government that has proved itself untrustworthy. Wars may be waged not in order to destroy an enemy society but to force the enemy to desist from the wrong in which he is engaged or about to engage. Spelling out the particular wrong which justifies one's taking up arms *eo ipso* spells out the conditions on which one ought to be ready to accept surrender.

War, then, must be waged in order to right a specific wrong: that is what gives one the right to go to war, the *ius ad bellum*. One has this right only if war is taken up as a last resort, when other measures of redressing the grievance or preventing aggression have failed. There must be good hope of victory: if there is not, the wrong which occasioned the war will not be righted thereby. The good to be obtained by the righting of the wrong must outweigh the harm which will be done by the choice of war as a means. Again, the harm done in war-making shall be no more than is necessary for achieving the legitimate goal of the war. Finally, if a war is to be just, one must not only have *ius ad bellum*, but observe *ius in bello*: that is to say, the rules of war must be observed in the combat itself.

The provisoes which I have specified derive from the reflections of philosophers and theologians on the conditions for a just war between the Middle Ages and the present century. The thinkers in question were mostly Christians, but there is nothing in their arguments which appeals to premises which are peculiar to Christian belief. Several of the rules which they laid down have been embodied from time to time in international agreements. Nations vilify their enemies when they violate the rules of war, and proudly proclaim the fact when they themselves observe them. The rules are not a set of arbitrary prohibitions. They are an articulation of the only conditions under which the international community can rationally accept war, in the absence of an effective supranational coercive force as a means of righting international wrongs. War is justifiable only if war can be limited, just as within a particular society police forces are necessary but are tolerable only if there are limits to their powers.

Killing the Innocent

The most important of the traditional conditions for a just war was that it should not involve the deliberate killing of noncombatants. This was sometimes called the prohibition on "killing the innocent", but the innocence in question had nothing to do with moral guiltlessness or lack of responsibility: the "innocent" were those who were not *nocentes* in the sense of engaged in harming one's own forces. Soldiers who had surrendered were, in this sense, no less "innocent" than infants in arms, and had an equal right to be spared. The traditional principle is best formulated thus: it is lawful to kill only those who are engaged in making war, or in supplying those waging war with the means of doing so.

The principle, thus formulated, does justify the deliberate killing of more than those who are wearing uniform. It regards as justified, for instance, the killing of munitions workers, or of civilians driving trainloads or truckloads of soldiers. The unintended deaths of uninvolved civilians resulting from an attack on a military target—for example, the blowing up of a castle or the bombing of a naval dockyard—were likewise not condemned as murderous by this principle, which was concerned with

10

deliberate killing, though of course they were something very relevant to the question of whether the war was doing more harm than good. What was clearly ruled out was the deliberate massacre of civilian populations or the devastation of whole cities as an end in itself or as a means to victory.

It is often said that the conditions for a just war were rules drawn up in a medieval context and are quite inapplicable in modern wars. It is certainly true that the rules are not always observed in contemporary wars; no more were they, for that matter, in the Middle Ages. But it is no objection to a moral principle to point out that people often break it: morals are about what we ought to do, not about what we in fact do. To say that the rules of war are out of date because people nowadays do not keep them is as absurd as to say that the law of contract is now superannuated because so many people shoplift. But a distinction can no longer be made between combatants and non-combatants, we are told, because nowadays war is total and the whole community is involved in total war. If what is meant by saying that war is total is that nowadays war is waged *by* whole communities, then it is untrue that any war is total: even at the point of maximum mobilisation in the Second World War a large part of the population of the warring nations consisted of children or those who were maintaining the services that would have been essential even in peacetime. If what is meant by saying that war is total is that nowadays war is waged *against* whole communities, this is unfortunately true. The relevant difference beween us and medieval society is that we have become technologically so much more proficient at doing this.

In fact the distinctions on which the rules of the just war were based were clearly applicable in the Second World War. The allies began the war with a cause which was clearly just: to right the wrong done to Poland in September 1939 and to prevent further aggression by an intrinsically evil political system. In the course of the war they violated the prohibition on mass killing of non-combatants. They did this not through any inability to notice a distinction between combatants and non-combatants but through a deliberate decision to ignore it. In the case of the United Kingdom, the decision to change from a policy of bombing military targets to a policy of the area bombing of centres of population was an explicit and bitterly contested decision at the highest level. In the case of the United States, the decision to use the first atom bombs to wipe out the cities of Hiroshima and Nagasaki was taken—on the most charitable version of events—on the basis of a cool calculation that the devastation of these centres of population was the speediest way of ensuring a victorious end to the war.

I have spent time sketching the just war tradition because I believe that it still provides the best theoretical framework within which to consider questions of right and wrong in warfare. It is the moral tradition which is spelt out in a number of Christian statements on nuclear issues, for instance the Anglican study *The Church and the Bomb* (Hodder & Stoughton, 1982) and the American Roman Catholic bishops' pastoral letter *The Challenge of Peace* of May 1983. It lies behind a number of classic statements of the international laws of war, for instance the Geneva Convention of 1949, which states:

> Persons taking no active part in the hostilities, including members of armed forces who have laid down their arms . . . shall in all circumstances be treated humanely. . .
> To this end, the following acts are and shall remain prohibited at any time and in any place whatsoever with respect to the above mentioned persons:
> (a) violence to life and person, in particular murder of all kinds, mutilation, cruel treatment and torture.

In a similar spirit, the Geneva Protocol of 1977 states:

> The civilians shall not be the object of attack. Acts or threats of violence the primary purpose of which is to spread terror among the civilian population are prohibited. . .
> Indiscriminate attacks are prohibited. Among others, the following types of attacks are to be considered as indiscriminate: an attack by bombardment by any methods or means which treats as a single military objective a number of clearly separated and distinct military objectives located in a city, town, village or other area containing a similar concentration of civilians or civilian objects; and an attack

which may be expected to cause incidental loss of civilian life . . . which would be excessive in relation to the concrete and direct military advantage anticipated.

At Nuremberg, when the Nazi war leaders were tried, they were accused of crimes against peace (violations of *ius ad bellum*) and war crimes (violations of *ius in bello*). Altogether, the just war tradition deserves the attention of everyone, Christian or not, who believes neither in pacifism nor in uncontrolled and limitless warfare.

How does the current defence strategy of the West measure up against the standards of just warfare? The purpose of the armaments, nuclear and conventional, of the Nato powers is, we are told, defence against potential aggression, particularly from the Soviet Union and the Warsaw Pact powers. Thus, for instance, a typical statement by President Reagan, to mark the thirty-fifth anniversary of the western alliance:

> The values that bind Nato together are not abstract concepts. Individual liberty, the rule of law, and respect for dignity of the individual are priceless and real. They have been handed down to us at enormous sacrifice of blood and treasure. They are the cement of the alliance and we can never take them for granted. . .
> The founding members of Nato pledged to safeguard the 'freedom, common heritage and civilisation of their peoples' and to consider an armed attack against any one of them an attack against them all. . . The bedrock of our alliance is our unshakable commitment to ensure our security through collective self-defence.
> (*The Times*, 6th March 1984)

The defence of the United States or of the countries of western Europe against an attack designed to end their independence and to subject them to communist rule would indeed, I believe, provide a just cause of war. The right of nations to defend themselves against armed attack by others is recognised by the United Nations charter, and the differences between the social order of the western allies and the political system of Soviet communism are matters important enough to provide the grounds for a just war. Western politicians' talk of "the free world" is inappropriate insofar as it suggests that it is only within the Soviet orbit that there are tyrannical systems. But there is no doubt that the countries of the Nato alliance in general enjoy freedoms which are denied to citizens of Warsaw Pact countries and that those freedoms are worth fighting to preserve. The many who have tried to escape from the East into the West have been prepared to risk their lives to achieve a share in those freedoms, and those of us who have been fortunate enough to enjoy them all our lives should surely be prepared to risk our lives to preserve them for ourselves and our successors.

In the event of an invasion by the Warsaw Pact powers, then, the West would have a legitimate cause of war. But would it be permissible to use nuclear weapons in such a war? The use of the first atom bombs on Hiroshima and Nagasaki was clearly in violation of the principles of just warfare. In each case the population of a city was taken as the target of an attack, with a view to terrorising the Japanese nation into surrender. It is true that the atomic attacks on Japanese cities had been preceded by even more devastating attacks on German cities by conventional means: it is not only nuclear weapons which can be used in morally unacceptable ways. What is special about nuclear weapons is that they are uniquely well adapted for the obliteration of populations.

Striking Back *No! Cost & justification is moral.*

Weapons considered merely as inert pieces of hardware are not, of course, objects of moral evaluation. It is the uses to which weapons are put, and the intentions and purposes of those who manufacture and deploy them, which are morally good or evil. For the earliest nuclear weapons, and for the largest and clumsiest of those still in the arsenals of the nuclear powers, it is difficult to conceive of any realistic use which will not involve the destruction of centres of population. Any such use would involve the killing of the innocent in terms of the just war tradition, and would be indiscriminate in the sense proscribed by the Geneva Protocol.

Throughout the vagaries of western nuclear strategy since

the 1950s, western leaders have always reserved the right, and often proclaimed the intention, sometimes euphemistically, of using their weapons to annihilate enemy cities and populations. When the use of atomic bombs first figured in American plans for war against the Soviet Union in 1947, it was stated that "Soviet urban industrial concentrations" were the "highest priority target system". When the hydrogen bomb was being developed in 1949, the American Atomic Energy Commission was advised:

> It is clear that the use of this weapon would bring about the destruction of innumerable human lives; it is not a weapon which can be used exclusively for the destruction of material installations of military or semi-military purposes. Its use therefore carries much further than the atomic bomb itself the policy of exterminating civilian populations.

Notwithstanding this advice, thermonuclear weapons were developed and became the keystone of John Foster Dulles's policy, in the Eisenhower administration of 1953, of "massive retaliation".

This policy called for the launching of all strategic forces on Soviet, Chinese and satellite cities on the initiation of nuclear war with the Soviet Union. When the Kennedy administration took over, it modified these plans, and, at a famous speech in Ann Arbor in 1962, Secretary of Defense Mr Robert McNamara explained the new counterforce strategy:

> Principal military objectives, in the event of a nuclear war stemming from a major attack on the alliance, should be the destruction of the enemy's military forces, not of his civilian population.

Mr McNamara's distinction between counterforce and counter-value strategies made clear that even in the nuclear age it was possible to draw the distinction between combatants and non-combatants which underlay the traditional prohibition on the killing of the innocent. But even in the moment of announcing the counterforce policy, he went on to say:

> The very strength and nature of the alliance forces makes it possible for us to retain, even in the face of a massive surprise attack, suf-

ficient reserve striking power to destroy an enemy society if driven to it.

And when only four months later it came to the Cuban missile crisis, Kennedy threatened a "full retaliatory strike".

The ultimate threat of wiping out a large part of an enemy society has remained the bedrock of American strategy from that day to this. Even in a book urging readers to halt the arms race and support a nuclear freeze, the authors, Senators Kennedy and Hatfield, say that "an all-out Soviet attack against the United States would precipitate massive retaliation by American nuclear forces against the Soviet Union". The book questions many of the assumptions of current American defence policy, yet the authors enunciate this as if it was not an assumption which in any way needed rethinking.

MAD

It is true that ever since the early 1960s there has been official dissatisfaction with the strategy of "Mutual Assured Destruction" (MAD). Successive secretaries of defense have sought to offer the American president, in the event of a nuclear crisis, some sort of third alternative to the two options of surrender and mutual obliteration. Robert McNamara set up a new targeting plan, known as the Single Integrated Operational Plan (SIOP) which organised selected packages of targets and provided for not firing on unselected ones, at least at an early stage of conflict. The aim was to limit damage to the American population by holding out an incentive to the Soviet Union, after an initial American attack, not to retaliate on cities for fear of a follow-on attack on its own population. Here too the ultimate rationale of the strategy was the holding of Soviet cities hostage to a final onslaught. In the 1970s, defense secretary Schlesinger built into the SIOP a number of smaller strikes at particular targets, for example the Soviet petroleum industry. This was in the hope that the exercise of limited nuclear options would influence the Russians during a nuclear war to come to the bargaining table to negotiate its termination before cities on either side had been destroyed. Nonetheless, according to General William Odom, who was an adviser to the National Security Council under President Carter, the SIOP of the 1970s offered the president only two choices in the event of nuclear attack, "releasing 70 – 80% of our nuclear megatonnage in one orgasmic whump, or just sitting there and saying: 'Don't do anything, and we will just take the incoming blow.'"

It was with a view to improving this situation that General Odom wrote a paper issued by President Carter as presidential directive PD-59, signed in July 1980. This, and the national security decision directive NSDD-13 of the Reagan administration which modified and slightly superseded it, called for plans to be made to enable the president to wage a protracted nuclear war. Both documents claim that the key to victory in a nuclear war with the Soviet Union is to target not just the military forces but the political and military control system.

The new strategy has been widely criticised. For all its suicidal dangers, it is argued, the strategy of MAD at least recognised that there could be no victors in a nuclear war, and offered deterrence as the only rationale for the possession of nuclear weapons. The strategy of PD-59, for all its benign emphasis on limiting damage in a nuclear war and avoiding direct attacks on populations, made it more likely that a nuclear war might actually be fought by holding out the idea that there could be victory. And while the menace to populations is removed from the forefront of peacetime strategy, the threat remains to be held over, and perhaps carried out on, the enemy during time of war. Thus American administrations can claim that in recent years cities have not been targeted as such, and yet it is widely believed that the final stage of the current SIOP, as of all its predecessors, involves attacks on Soviet "recovery" targets, concentrations of property and human institutions which might allow the Soviet Union to rebuild after the war.

The strategy of the independent British deterrent has been simpler. The 1981 *Statement on the Defence Estimates* spoke of the need for the strategic nuclear force to be "capable of posing a convincing threat—of inflicting, on key aspects of Soviet state power, damage which any Soviet leadership would regard as out of all proportion to any likely gains from aggression against us". Behind the euphemism "key aspects of Soviet state power" lies the threat of an attack on Soviet centres of population. Targeting policy is officially secret, but the 64 missiles of the British Polaris submarine force, each with 3,200 kiloton warheads, are ill-adapted for purposes other than the destruction of Moscow and other major Soviet cities on which they can unleash the explosive power of some 3,000 Hiroshimas.

The Gravest Crime

If politicians and strategists have remained committed to a last resort policy of attacks on populations, there has been in the past 40 years a growing acceptance by moralists and religious thinkers that such attacks cannot be justified by any rational ethics of war. Thus the fathers of the Second Vatican Council, assembled from all the countries of the Catholic world, proclaimed:

> Any act of war aimed indiscriminately at the destruction of entire cities or of extensive areas along with their population is a crime against God and humanity itself. It merits unequivocal and unhesitating condemnation.

Following this lead, the American Catholic bishops in their pastoral letter of May 1983 stated:

> Under no circumstances may nuclear weapons or other instruments of mass slaughter be used for the purpose of destroying population centres or other predominantly civilian targets

and they drew the conclusion: "No Christian can rightfully carry out orders or policies deliberately aimed at killing non-combatants." The Church of England report, *The Church and the Bomb*, drew from the same principles a wider conclusion:

> It is in our view proven beyond reasonable doubt that the just war theory, as this has developed in western civilisation and within the Christian Church, rules out the use of nuclear weapons. The damage to non-combatants, even indeed to neutral countries as unconnected

with the quarrel as they are distant from the scene of operations; the havoc made of the environment; and the dangers to generations yet unborn: these things make nuclear weapons indiscriminate and nuclear war almost inevitably disproportionate.

A resolution of the general assembly of the United Nations in 1981 declared the first use of nuclear weapons to be "the gravest crime against humanity", and claimed that there could never by any justification for authorising their first use.

The conviction that it is wrong to base a strategy on plans to destroy populations is not one that is peculiar to pacific churchmen. Colin S. Gray, of the National Institute for Public Policy of Fairfax, Virginia, has written an article "War-fighting for Deterrence" (*The Journal of Strategic Studies*, March 1984) in which he castigates Secretary of Defense Mr Caspar Weinberger for being insufficiently committed to the pursuit of victory in nuclear war. In the course of that article Gray writes:

> In the moral dimension—no matter what good may be intended to prevent war from occurring—this author, in company with the National Conference of Catholic Bishops, believes it is absolutely wrong either to attack civilian noncombatant targets deliberately, or even to threaten such.

(Such a policy is not only immoral, Gray believes, but also unnecessary. The Soviet leaders place so much higher value on their own power of coercive control than they do on the civilian society of the Soviet Union that a counterforce attack is a much more deterrent prospect than a countervalue one. There was no need, therefore, for McNamara in 1962 to hold out the prospect of the ultimate destruction of society as a follow-up to the counterforce target plan.)

The Ethics of Retaliation

It is the first use of nuclear weapons on centres of population which is seen by many as a paradigmatically wicked act of war. What, though, of other uses of nuclear weapons? Do they all fall under the same condemnation?

Retaliatory attacks on cities are wrong for the same reasons as the initiation of such attacks. It is the killing of the innocent which is wrong, not just the unprovoked killing of the innocent: two wrongs do not make a right. It is legitimate in self-defence to use force which would not be legitimate if one were not being attacked, but retaliation is not self-defence. Nor could the retaliatory attacks be justified as punishment: only a fraction of the citizens to be killed in such an attack could bear responsibility for the reckless acts of their government which had provoked the retaliation.

Retaliation on Soviet cities might be considered by an American president in two different circumstances: after an initial Russian counterforce attack, causing considerable collateral damage, or after a full-scale onslaught in which America's own cities had been wiped out. In the first case, it might be thought that prudence would restrain retaliation because of the American cities that are still hostage to the remaining Russian missiles. This, after all, is the mirror image of the effect an American flexible response is supposed to have on Russian decision-makers. But Gray, in the article quoted, expresses himself doubtful of this:

> One can show, with impressive strategic logic, that even a United States capable of launching under or after attack should find that it is deterred from exercising its deterrent because of the amount that would remain to be lost. However this author is firmly convinced that no American president would sit still for 2m to 50m American prompt fatalities. Regardless of strategic reasoning, the president . . . would order a volley to be fired back for the sake of national honour or even just to satisfy the primitive motive of revenge. Millions of dead Americans would constitute a debt of blood to be repaid, inappropriate and even fatal though such repayment might prove to be.

If a scholar can write in such terms in the calm of a peacetime study, it is all too likely that a president might be swayed by such motives in the stress and haste of wartime decisions. And if a president would order retaliation even with so much still at risk, how much more likely is it that he would do so after absorbing a full-scale nuclear attack where it might well appear that there was nothing more left to lose?

But would it be rational to launch a retaliatory strike if one had suffered the unimaginable horrors of a full-scale nuclear war? Otherwise than as an act of revenge, a retaliatory strike would seem to be at best pointless, and indeed against the striker's own interest, considered from even the most strictly selfish point of view. A second strike would have no deterrent effect: it would by this time be too late for deterrence to have any force. It would not be like the punishing of criminals within a local society, too late indeed to prevent the crime which is being punished, but calculated to teach a lesson to the individual criminal for the next time, and to the other citizens for the future. It would act against the interest of the striking nation because it would decrease the possibility of those who remained as survivors receiving the medical assistance and economic aid which they would need if they were to rebuild anything of their stricken society.

The differences which at present exist between the United States and the Soviet Union would be insignificant in comparison with the difference between the United States as it now is and the United States as it would be after absorbing a full-scale nuclear attack, or the differences between the Soviet Union as it now is and the Soviet Union as it would be after such an attack. From the point of view of material civilisation and technology, once America and its allies had suffered a nuclear attack, the nearest thing there would be to the orginal United States would be the as yet undestroyed industrial society of the Soviet Union, and it would be this hostile but kindred society which would provide the best hope, in the long run, of any eventual reconstruction of the United States, akin to the rehabilitation of Germany and Japan by the allied powers after the Second World War. From the non-material point of view, of course, after the United States had absorbed a nuclear attack from the Soviet Union it would have an enormous moral advantage over its enemy in that it was not—yet—guilty of mass-murder on a scale unparalleled in history. But *that* advantage is precisely what it would throw away, in a matter of minutes, by launching a retaliatory attack. And it would be thrown away without the slightest prospective material advantage in return.

Even from the point of view of self-interest, then, massive retaliation would be irrational. From the moral point of view, it would simply be murder. I am using the word not as a term of abuse but in the precise sense in which the killing of the innocent as an end in itself or as a means to one's ends has always been regarded as murder. (The word "innocent" in the traditional definition was meant to exclude two classes of people who might justifiably be killed: enemy combatants in battle, and those convicted of a capital crime in one's own jurisdiction.) There is no doubt that a counter-city strategy in a nuclear war would involve the deliberate killing of the innocent, and therefore be murder by the traditional rules of the just war.

Murder is never justified. If an action clearly falls within the definition of murder, then it is not a morally permissible option. It is something which should be ruled out in advance, not something the pros and cons of which should be weighed up in the particular case. In saying this I am disagreeing with those moralists and strategists of a utilitarian or consequentialist frame of mind who refuse to rule out, in advance, indiscriminate attacks on populations. Such thinkers, in order to make a moral judgment about a massacre of that kind, would demand to know what, in the concrete circumstances, was the good to be achieved or the evil to be avoided by such an attack. I believe that such a moral approach is perniciously mistaken. There is indeed a large field of human intercourse and endeavour where actions are to be decided on in the light of their likely consequences. But such deliberation, such investigation into means towards desirable ends, must take place within a framework in which certain evil means are ruled out absolutely. For we know that certain means are evil much more clearly than we know that certain ends are good, and when we do evil that good may come, we are much more certain of the evil we do than the good we hope for. If we are told that a certain policy or course of action involves genocide, or murder, or torture, or enslavement, we should not ask: "And what good will it do?" We should have nothing further to do with it.

Massive nuclear attacks, then, on centres of population, or on the industrial bases of an enemy society, or on command and control centres situated in densely populated areas, cannot be regarded as legitimate steps towards the winning of a war, or even the "prevailing" in a war or the "bringing a war to a termination on favourable terms", to use some of the recent euphemisms of strategists who have accepted that in a nuclear war there is no such thing as a victory. But what of uses of nuclear weapons for purposes other than the destruction of cities and populations? Certainly, not every imaginable use of nuclear weapons need involve the slaughter of the innocent. An attack on an army on the move in an unpopulated area, or a strategic strike on missile silos far away from civil habitation, would not necessarily violate the principle of non-combatant immunity in warfare. So it is possible to think of legitimate targets for even large-scale nuclear weapons, though their use even on such targets might well have unacceptable consequences through fall-out and long-term climatic effects. When we consider weapons at the lower end of the nuclear scale, it is quite easy to envisage realistic military uses which, in themselves, are quite legitimate: the use of a nuclear depth-charge upon a nuclear submarine would surely be an impeccable exercise in war-making, considered in isolation from any more general strategic context. Does this mean that provided deliberate attacks on cities are avoided, a nuclear war can be justified?

3 Limited Nuclear War

Strategists in Washington's Pentagon and Whitehall's Ministry of Defence sometimes maintain that there could be such a thing as a limited nuclear war: a war which could be brought to a successful end after a nuclear artillery exchange in Europe, or an intercontinental counterforce strike, without leading to a strategic exchange or involving deliberate attacks on cities taking populations as targets. There is usually some unclarity about what is meant by bringing such a nuclear war to a successful conclusion, or terminating it on advantageous terms. But without probing this unclarity, let us ask whether such a war would be a morally acceptable option.

Here there are two principal questions to be asked. The first is whether, on the assumption that the war remains as limited as the strategists envisage, it would be in itself a morally acceptable option. The second is whether it is likely that a nuclear war, once begun, could be kept under control and remain within the limits which were planned at the outset. Both questions are relevant to the moral evaluation of limited nuclear warfare.

Let us remember that in civil life a killer can be convicted of murder even though he did not intend to kill his victim. A man can be a murderer even though his victim's death was neither one of his purposes nor a means which he had chosen to achieve his ends. A death which is foreseen but not intended can amount to murder if the killer's action demonstrates, as the lawyers say, a reckless disregard for human life. Such disregard might be shown, for instance, by a failure to take precautions

24

while engaged in a lethally dangerous activity, or it might be inferred from the triviality of the goal pursued by potentially lethal means. Though not every action which results in a fore-seen but unintended death is murderous, such disregard for human life can turn unintended killing into murder.

Similarly, in wartime it would not be sufficient to rebut a charge of murder if one could show that one's use of weapons was aimed at, and had the sole purpose of, destroying a military target. For the weapons might unintentionally cause a number of civilian casualties wholly out of proportion to the military goal to be achieved. That is why among the rules for the just war which govern *ius in bello* there is, in addition to the condition of non-combatant immunity, a condition of proportionality. In war as in peace murder can be committed not only intention-ally, but also recklessly, not only when civilian deaths are the purpose of a strike, as in terror bombing, but also when they are the unintended but disproportionate result of the strike. This might be the case if a one-megaton bomb was dropped on Moscow to wipe out a command and control centre there.

Not every unintended death of a civilian following an attack on a military target counts as murder. As we said earlier, an attack on a barracks may be justified even if it leads to the death of the cleaners and canteen workers. It is reckless killing that is under consideration, and here there is room for the weighing of costs and benefits. That is why the principle here is one of proportionality. But disproportionate civilian casualties can make an attack on a military target as murderous as an attack on a city. Lord Zuckerman, the former chief government scientific adviser in the United Kingdom, is on record as saying: "It is still inevitable that were military installations rather than cities to become the objective of nuclear attack, millions, even tens of millions of civilians would be killed whatever the pro-portion of missile sites, airfields, armament plants, ports and so on that would be destroyed." If this is so, then it seems that an attack of this kind on military targets in the central European theatre would count as reckless murder.

What this would mean in practice is not easy to visualise for those of us who do not know the likely disposition of Warsaw Pact forces and who are relatively unfamiliar with the geography of East Germany and Czechoslovakia. It is much easier to envisage what a policy of nuclear attack on military targets would mean if we look at it from an opposing point of view, and consider a hostile attack on military targets in the United Kingdom. According to figures published in the British Medical Association report (see page 4), a counterforce attack of 222mt on the United Kingdom, targeted primarily on military targets but with some industrial centres also targeted, could produce a total of over 38m deaths. This would leave almost as many dead as a deliberate attempt to wipe out the population. The principal difference would be that a counterforce attack would need to use a larger number of warheads with relatively low yields, so that the number of deaths from blast would decrease while the number of deaths from fall-out would increase. If Nato's target map of eastern Europe looks at all like a Soviet target map of Britain, then a corresponding western attack on Soviet forces would involve the death of the greater part of the population between the Elbe and the Vistula.

The British Medical Association figures were calculated before the arrival of cruise missiles in Britain. Cruise missiles are designed to be mobile, and to be fired from launching platforms dispersed through the country. Once deployed away from their base they are difficult to detect and destroy. According to a parliamentary reply by the Secretary of State for Defence in 1981, more than 1,000mt would be needed to destroy the ground-launched cruise missiles once they were deployed. A Soviet spokesman stated that a likely military response to the deployment would be to redeploy the 25mt warheads of the obsolescent SS-9 intercontinental ballistic missiles for pattern-bombardment of the missile dispersal areas. A 600mt attack for this purpose would, of course, be sufficient to wipe out almost the entire population as a by-product of the elimination of the danger to the Soviet Union from the deployed missiles. No doubt similar carnage would be the consequence of any western attempt to destroy the mobile SS-20s of the Soviet intermediate theatre force, now deployed in Germany and Czechoslovakia. It is clear that such an attack by either side would be reckless murder, however much each side would claim that the other had brought the attack on itself by its deployment of the missiles.

Crossing the Firebreak

It is possible to imagine military uses of nuclear weapons on a much less devastating scale. A Lance missile has a range of 75 miles, is accurate to within about 50 yards, and may have a yield of a mere 10kt. The use in isolation of one of these on a massive tank formation at the rear of attacking Warsaw Pact troops might be argued to be within the bounds of proportionate military force. To use more than a fraction of the 500 stockpiled might quickly take us beyond the bounds: even a single one has a yield that approaches that of the Hiroshima atom bomb. But that is not the most serious objection to the limited nuclear strike which would be represented by the use of Lance alone. If Lance was all that Nato possessed by way of nuclear weapons, then the use of them could be judged on its own merits. But against the background threat of Pershing, Poseidon and Minuteman, the use of Lance must be seen as a step on an escalatory ladder and as such is a very different matter. In the familiar metaphor, the use even of a single Lance would involve crossing the firebreak between nuclear and non-nuclear weapons, and the size of the danger of crossing the firebreak depends on the size of the fire-risk on the opposite side of the divide.

In present circumstances, the crossing of the firebreak appears to be an unacceptable risk. There can, of course, be no certainty that a limited use of nuclear weapons would lead to full-scale nuclear war. In a matter where human decisions intervene, there cannot be expert scientific prediction as there can about the medical effects of nuclear bombardment. But there can be prudent estimation of the likely outcome; and, in the estimation of many well placed to make a judgment, the likelihood of nuclear war remaining limited is slender.

From a number of impressive witnesses, I will cite three texts. Lord Mountbatten, former Chief of British Defence Staff, in a speech at Strasbourg in 1979, spoke of the introduction of tactical weapons:

> The belief was that were hostilities ever to break out in western Europe, such weapons could be used in field warfare without triggering an all-out nuclear exchange leading to the final holocaust. I have never found this idea credible . . . I repeat in all sincerity that as a military man I can see no use for any nuclear weapons which would not end in escalation, with consequences that no one can conceive.

Harold Brown, President Carter's Secretary of Defense, in his annual report for the financial year 1979, wrote thus:

> A full-scale thermonuclear exchange would be an unprecedented disaster for the Soviet Union as well as for the United States. Nor is it at all clear that an initial use of nuclear weapons—however selectively they might be targeted—could be kept from escalating to a full-scale thermonuclear exchange, especially if command and control centres were brought under attack. The odds are high, whether weapons were used against tactical or strategic targets, that control would be lost on both sides and the exchange would become unconstrained.

Best known of all is the article in *Foreign Affairs* in 1982 by four American administrators who had been involved in strategic and political decisions at the highest level: McGeorge Bundy, George Kennan, Robert McNamara and G. Smith:

> No one has ever succeeded in advancing any persuasive reason to believe that any use of nuclear weapons, even on the smallest scale, could reliably be expected to remain limited. Every serious analysis and every military exercise for over 25 years has demonstrated that even the most restrained battlefield use would be enormously destructive to civilian life and property. .". The only clearly definable firebreak against the world-wide disaster of general nuclear war is the one that stands between all other kinds of conflict and any use whatsoever of nuclear weapons. To keep that firebreak wide and strong is in the deepest interest of all mankind."

In 1982 Field-Marshal Lord Carver, former Chief of British Defence Staff, stated that first use of nuclear weapons by Nato would be "criminally irresponsible" because it could trigger a Soviet reaction that would destroy the West. Former American defense secretary Melvin Laird agreed with him. And in 1983 McNamara, in an article in *Newsweek*, reaffirmed his belief that if Nato initiated the use of nuclear weapons it would almost certainly lead to the destruction of western civilisation.

In spite of these warnings, Nato continues to reserve the right to make first use of nuclear weapons if its conventional forces should be in danger of defeat from a Soviet invasion of western Europe. Defenders of this policy often concede that the use of tactical nuclear weapons would not serve any military purpose in the sense of bringing victory closer in the actual battle engaged. But they would be, it is argued, an expression of political will, which would act on the political will of the enemy and cause him to pause before proceeding further with his aggression.

We must ask: "What is the political will which the tactical use of nuclear weapons would express?" If it is the willingness to proceed up the ladder of escalation to the point of strategic exchange, then such tactical use is simply a particularly clangorous expression of willingness to wage an all-out suicidal war. But whether or not this is so, the firing of a "warning shot" in this way is likely to be ineffective, and extremely dangerous. If the Russians have reached a point where they are willing to invade western Europe, they must already have considered, and discounted, the Nato threat of first tactical use. They are unlikely, therefore, to stop in their tracks when that threat is carried out. There must also be a serious possibility that they will carry out their own declared threat of responding to Nato's tactical use with a massive attack on European if not American centres of strategic power. And such an attack would be likely to carry with it the destruction of much of Britain.

Defenders of Nato first use argue that a massive Soviet response is uncertain, and perhaps even unlikely. *Ex hypothesi* the

Warsaw Pact troops against whom the weapons were used would be aggressors engaged in foreign adventures. The threat of nuclear strike dramatised by the first use of tactical weapons, on the other hand, is a threat against Soviet homelands and in defence of western homelands. Hence there is an assymetry of interest, which is likely to give the Soviet aggressor pause. Nato first use, then, may serve the purpose of checking a conventional invasion without involving an unacceptable risk of all-out war.

Against this, it must be pointed out that the assymetry of interest is not likely to be present in the most probable scenario for a Soviet invasion, namely, where the purpose of a strike into western Europe is to neutralise Nato nuclear installations. Nuclear weapons are not just a means of waging war for other goals: they provide, in the present world situation, the most potent prizes of victory and incentives to war. The wish to get rid of an opponent's nuclear threat—such as the Soviet Union's missiles in Cuba—provides the only realistic motive for risking nuclear warfare. A Soviet force which had engaged upon an incursion into western Europe for this purpose would believe that it was fighting to protect its own homeland no less than if it was fighting inch by inch across the steppes against an incoming Napoleon or Hitler. So we cannot comfort ourselves with the thought that after a Nato first nuclear strike, escalation would be prevented by the assymetry of interest between aggressor and defender.

It is indeed just possible that after a first use of nuclear weapons escalation might be halted. But this mere possibility is not enough to justify such a use. The American Catholic bishops, recognising the uncertainties, were surely right to conclude that the presumption was against the legitimacy of crossing the boundary between conventional and nuclear war:

> To cross this divide is to enter a world where we have no experience of control, much testimony against its possibility, and therefore no justification for submitting the human community to this risk.

Their judgment had been anticipated in the General Synod of the Church of England in February 1983 where the following motion was adopted:

> This Synod . . . judges that even a small-scale first use of nuclear
> weapons could never be morally justified in view of the high risk
> that this would lead to full-scale nuclear warfare.

Attacking the Rules of War

If large-scale nuclear warfare, then, involves deliberate killing
of the innocent, and if the initiation of small-scale war involves a
recklessness which would make the initiator responsible for the
resulting deaths of non-combatants, it seems that it is difficult
to justify, by the traditional criteria of the just war, any of the
uses of nuclear weapons envisaged in current western strategy.
Someone who wishes to defend that strategy must therefore
attack the rules of war.

Some may do so on the general ground that moral rules are
unhelpful: the way to decide what is right is to weigh up the
good and bad consequences of what you are considering, and do
what is likely to have the best overall outcome, even if this
violates long-cherished rules and conventions. This kind of
thoroughgoing utilitarianism is, fortunately, commoner in text-
books of moral philosophy than in real life. Outside their studies
even philosophers are unlikely to proclaim that they will literally
stop at nothing to achieve goals they believe to be desirable.
Others may maintain that while moral rules may be all right in
peacetime, they are out of place during a war, or that moral
rules apply to individuals but not to governments. No one in
fact consistently believes this. We complain when our enemies
violate the rules of war, we blame the Nazis for what they did in
wartime as well as in peacetime, and for what they did as a
government and not just as individuals. All of us, including
armaments manufacturers, expect governments no less than
the citizen to honour their contracts and settle their bills.

It is more common to attack the specific conditions for a just
war. They are medieval and out of date, we are told; they are no
more to be observed than feudal dues or the laws against usury.
The argument goes that it is impossible nowadays to distin-

guish between combatants and non-combatants; in conditions of total war there is no distinction between guilty and innocent. Wars are nowadays fought between entire populations, and all are responsible. This claim is particularly implausible in the context of the struggle between East and West. Among the likely victims of a nuclear exchange would be the inhabitants of the Soviet satellites. Can it be seriously maintained that the entire peoples of Poland and Czechoslovakia are to be held responsible for the actions of the alien tyranny under which they are unfortunate enough to have to suffer? But in any case, as was said above, the prohibition on killing the innocent in war has nothing to do with moral guiltlessness or lack of responsibility. If it did, we would have more reason than the population of eastern Europe to tremble at the prospect of just retribution. We have more responsibility for the governments whom we elect, and against whom we can protest without fear of imprisonment, than they have for the regimes imposed on them from outside and maintained by draconian policing.

There are those who argue that, while a nuclear war would not be justified against the present Soviet Union, there are imaginable circumstances in which waging such a war would be legitimate as the choice of a lesser evil. Hitler, for instance, was an evil tyrant who caused a war which involved the loss of 50m lives. Would it not have been right, if we had had atomic weapons in time to prevent Hitler's aggression, to have used them against Germany to prevent the greater evil which in fact transpired?

I am not sure whether this argument is meant to justify the conclusion that against some future neo-Hitler we would be justified in launching a nuclear war provided that it cost something under 50m lives. It seems open to doubt whether it would be, in fact, a lesser evil to be a victim in a nuclear war on that scale rather than brought under a Hitlerian yoke. But let us suppose for the sake of argument that it would. When we speak of a choice between evils, we have to make a distinction between evils that we do and evils that we have to put up with. It seems sensible and sound to say that if faced with two evils, you must choose the lesser. But it is important to understand this principle correctly if it is not to lapse into the justification of doing evil that good may come. If you cannot avoid doing either A or B, and if both of these are evils, then it is true that you should do whichever of the two is less bad. But doing A which is bad, in case someone else does B which is worse, is not a case of choosing the lesser evil. It is simply a case of doing evil that good may come, and this is not something which is morally acceptable: the end does not justify the means.

The spectre of Hitler is often raised in order to justify preparation for nuclear war, both in the western democracies and in the Soviet Union. The issue has been well dealt with in a German dialogue written by the philosopher Ernst Tugendhat, *Rationalität und Irrationalität der Friedensbewegung und ihrer Gegner* (Europäische Perspektiven GmbH, 1983). At one point, one of the characters is presenting the argument that the risk of Soviet domination does not justify the threat of nuclear war:

> Consider how many countries are already under the domination of the Soviet Union today. This is something we accept. Consider that terror and torture reign in many other countries connected with our own western system. This is something we tolerate and indirectly even support. Consider further that in large parts of the world millions of people die every year of hunger. This too is something we tolerate, though it need not be the case if it were not for our armaments. Why then should we choose to threaten not only our enemy and ourselves, but the whole of humanity with destruction, simply to avert the possibility that we might be threatened by a fate which would be no worse than those we tolerate for others?

In reply to this, the interlocutor says: "I want to put a final question to see whether your argument is a principled one. Assume that you are not dealing with the Soviet Union, but with the Nazis. What would your view be then?" Tugendhat's spokesman replies that to defeat the Nazis he would be prepared to kill and risk his life, but that even against the Nazis there must be limits to what one does:

> Try to visualise the actual situation in the concrete. Think of all the

most terrible things we associate with the Nazis, and imagine that that situation obtains today in eastern Europe. Now as then, people are herded together in towns and villages and mown down with machine guns. Now as then, the gas chambers operate. And shall we liberate eastern Europe by threatening and if necessary starting a nuclear war? Just consider that in the holocaust which then would threaten, those of us who did not die immediately would beg those who still had weapons to shoot us and our children. If the gas chambers still existed we would line up of our own free will in front of their gates.

Better Dead than Red

There are those in this country who regard Soviet communists with just as much horror as the Nazis have ever been regarded, and regard a nuclear war as less of a disaster than subjection to the Soviet yoke. Thus, a correspondent in *The Times* on 25th October 1982 wrote as follows:

> I would say (on behalf of myself, if not God or humanity) that it is preferable to risk blowing the world to kingdom come than to accept a hegemony imposed on the United Kingdom by external didacts, whether Russian or Martian. Better dead than red.

"Better dead than red" is a slogan which has several meanings. If it means that one should risk one's life rather than submit to communism, then it expresses a sentiment which is shared by all those who, like myself, believe that it would be right to fight and die in a conventional war against a communist invasion. Some might go further, and believe that one should die rather than submit to communist rule. Someone might hold this in the extreme form of believing that one should kill oneself rather than fall into communist hands. I believe this to be a mistaken moral judgment, but I would not wish to argue with those who hold it. They can, when the time comes, act upon their principles without involving us or anyone else in war, nuclear or otherwise, in the meantime.

But it is in a different sense that, as in the passage above, the slogan "better dead than red" is most often used to justify western nuclear policy. The differences between the communist system and our own are such, it is maintained, that to prevent the evil of having communism imposed upon us we would be justified not only in going to war, but in waging a war which would violate the traditional rules for the conduct of wars: a war of mass destruction and indiscriminate killing. Better for every-one—both on our side and on theirs—to be made dead than for us to be made red by having communism forced upon us.

I am at pains to elucidate the senses of "better dead than red" in which it contains some truth because in this, the important sense, it enshrines a monstrous falsehood. The differences between the West and the Warsaw Pact nations are of two kinds, material and non-material. Western nations enjoy a number of material advantages over their eastern counterparts, advantages which can be summed up by saying that we have in general a higher standard of living. More importantly, in the West we enjoy a large number of freedoms which are denied to those living in the Soviet bloc, and which facilitate the pursuit of many values which we cherish.

Nuclear attack on an enemy population is not justified by the defence of either of these advantages. Perhaps few would seriously maintain that one can justify inflicting a horrible death on millions poorer than oneself in order to protect the differential between one's standards of living. But the defence of western non-material values is equally impotent to provide a justification for nuclear massacre. Respect for innocent human life and for international law is as much a part of what gives us a right to defend the values of western democracy as is freedom of speech or rights against arbitrary arrest. To the extent to which we forfeit our respect for life and law we forfeit our claim to have any moral superiority to defend against communist threat. As for democratic institutions, few of these are likely to survive a war in which both sides suffer nuclear devastation. To keep life going at all after such a catastrophe is likely to demand a social organisation more ruthlessly authoritarian than anything now to be found on either side of the east-west divide. Even if the West by some miracle escaped devastation so that the massacre was one-sided, it would end the war having, by its own act, destroyed the claim that it possessed a system of human values which was worth fighting and dying for. Its institutions would deserve no more respect or loyalty than those of Hitler's Germany.

This is something which is being recognised more and more widely. Colin Gray, the spokesman for the American strategic right wing, has this to say in the article discussed on page 19:

> It would seem to be virtually self-evident that a country like the United States that has a founding state ideology of commitment to the life, liberty and pursuit of happiness of individual Americans, cannot credibly threaten to initiate an "exchange" of nuclear strikes against essentially civilian targets. As an operational strategy for compellent effect, such an idea affronts American values both in the sense of an absolute ethic (targeting non-combatants is morally wrong) and in the sense of an ethic of consequences (it would licence an intolerable attack on American society).

"Better dead than red" may, of course, be used to express a sentiment which is not a moral judgment at all, but merely a personal preference. If someone tells me that he would prefer to be a victim of a nuclear attack than be subject to Russian hegemony, I would not claim the right to disbelieve him. But such a preference can hardly be very widely shared. The inhabitants of Warsaw already suffer what we would have to suffer if we surrendered to Russian blackmail. Yet in the worst days of martial law, can anyone really believe that what the Polish people wanted was for the West to put them out of their agony by dropping a nuclear device upon the centre of Warsaw?

II. THE LOGIC OF DETERRENCE

4 Threat and Execution

Many people would agree with the argument so far, and accept that there can be no justification for actually fighting a nuclear war. Even a government pamphlet setting out to defend the British independent deterrent begins by saying: "Talk of fighting a nuclear war is dangerous nonsense, because there can be no winners in such a conflict." It is a good thing, however, that there is a spate of books describing the horrors of nuclear war, for it is necessary to keep reminding people of what the world would be like afterwards in order to bring home that there is no desirable goal which can rationally be pursued by launching such a war.

At this point the debate about nuclear weapons becomes really serious and difficult. Some say: "These weapons can never be used in a war that would be sane or moral, therefore we should get rid of them." Others say: "We must keep and modernise these weapons as a deterrent, because this is the only safe way to prevent the outbreak of a nuclear war which we all agree would be an ultimate disaster." Thus the pamphlet quoted in the paragraph above says: "The strategy of deterrence has held firm, despite the increasing international tensions of recent years, because it would be madness for either side to launch an attack on the other."

If that is how the strategy of deterrence is enunciated, there seems a paradox at its core. If A tries to deter B from something by threatening to launch a nuclear attack on B, A is threatening to do something which on A's own account it would be madness

37

for him to do. If B thinks that A means what he says, B must think that A is mad; if B thinks A does not mean what he says, then B must think that A is bluffing. Either way, then, B must think that A is either mad or lying, so how is A's threat supposed to provide a reason for B to act or to desist from action?

Perhaps when the British government says that it would be madness for either side to launch an attack on the other, what it really means is that it would be madness to initiate a nuclear attack on the other side, thus inviting nuclear retaliation. A second strike in retaliation for an attack on the other side is perhaps not, in the view of the government, something which is to be regarded as a piece of madness. It is this readiness for a second strike which provides the deterrent to an attack from the Soviet side.

Perhaps it is not quite as mad to retaliate when one has already suffered devastation as it is to attack first and invite annihilation. From a moral point of view, there is little to choose between the first attacker and the second, since two wrongs do not make a right. And it would not in fact, so I have argued, even be rational from the point of view of self-interest for a country which has undergone a nuclear attack to launch a retaliatory strike. Nonetheless, it is worth examining more closely the structure of the strategy of deterrence.

There are those who agree with the main conclusion of the previous chapter that nuclear war waged on populations or causing disproportionate numbers of civilian deaths is morally unacceptable, but who accept with various qualifications the policy of possessing and deploying nuclear weapons as a deterrent. It is with that position that I shall be concerned in the present section of my argument.

Those who, while renouncing full-scale nuclear war, defend nuclear deterrence, fall into two classes. There are those who justify possession of nuclear weapons as a deterrent on the grounds that some uses of those weapons may be legitimate, and there are those who defend the possession of nuclear weapons as a deterrent while agreeing that the use of them in all circumstances must be wrong.

I have already agreed that it is possible to imagine uses for at least some nuclear weapons which would be legitimate. Considered in themselves, none of the traditional criteria for the conduct of just war would rule out the interception of ballistic missiles, the use of nuclear depth-charges on submarines, or the explosion of a nuclear weapon as a demonstration shot in an uninhabited area. In concrete circumstances, of course, such activities might be intolerably provocative or dangerous, and might well be intended as an expression of a resolve to proceed to more nefarious uses of nuclear weapons; but in the abstract they are morally defensible. But it would be folly to conclude that because some uses of some nuclear weapons are legitimate, that makes all possession of any nuclear weapons legitimate. The legitimacy of the possession of nuclear weapons depends on the purposes for which they are kept and the likely ways in which they would be used. The defenders of deterrence do not claim that deterrence can be maintained by the threat of these marginal uses alone.

The crucial question is this. Is there any use of nuclear weapons which is both ethically justified and sufficiently extensive to underpin the deterrent threat? Can a potential aggressor be deterred by a threat to do anything less than launch a murderous attack? Or must it be the case that any threat which is sufficient to act as a deterrent to our potential enemies must be a threat whose execution would be immoral?

Morality and the Nuclear Threat

Before discussing this question we may begin by agreeing readily that the nuclear powers are in a position to inflict intolerable damage on an adversary without making use of all the capacity they possess: in order to deter they do not need to threaten to wage war to the limit of their strength. The superpowers could execute a deterrent threat with only a fraction of their present arsenals: this is one of the most frequent complaints of critics of the arms race. Even a minor nuclear power like the

United Kingdom has the physical power to cause, with a single one of its Polaris submarines, damage on a scale which no Soviet government is likely to think tolerable.

But to say that the damage which a deterrent threatens is less than a deterrer could inflict if unrestrained does not settle the question of whether such a threat of damage is justified. The Polaris warheads, for instance, in order to carry out a threat adequate to deter the Soviet Union, would have to be targeted on cities or military targets in densely populated areas. If the argument of the previous part of this book is accepted, the execution of such a threat could never be justified.

Defenders of the deterrent argue that a targeting strategy sufficient to deter need not involve any massive attacks on cities as such. An attack aimed at wrecking economic effort, transport systems and structures of command, in conjunction with a discriminating bombardment of forces in the field, could well cripple an aggressive regime in wartime and sap its will for military adventure, while leaving the great majority of its population intact. Even such an attack would, beyond doubt, cause a large number of non-combatant deaths; but these deaths would neither be the purpose of the attack nor out of proportion to the presumed goal of warding off totalitarian conquest with the slavery and deaths which this would bring in its train. In absolute terms, the number of deaths could well be substantially less than the number thought tolerable in the war against Hitler.

Hence, it is argued, there could be a scale of strike large enough to rob an aggressor of the will to continue a war, and yet limited enough so that the expected harm to civilians is less than the evil expected if the aggression is successful. It is no doubt difficult to decide in advance, and in ignorance of the exact nature of the aggressor and scale of the aggression, the precise target-plan and mix of weapons of different yields required for such a judicious onslaught. But its possibility is sufficient to justify the maintenance of the capability to administer such a blow should the occasion arise.

This argument may be presented in two forms. In one form, the argument goes that it is essential to the credibility of a deterrent that it should be accompanied by a thought-out and credible war-fighting plan, whether or not the plan was ever to be put into operation in the event of deterrence failing. In the other form, it is suggested that it might actually make sense to carry out such a plan in action. It could not, it is admitted, be carried out without huge non-combatant casualties, even though such casualties would not be the aim of the action. When it came to the point, the moral decision would have to be made by weighing these unsought casualties gravely in the balance against the desired political objectives of the war, seeking honestly to decide whether the objective sought was in proportion to the undesired but inevitable damage to innocent life. It may be that in practice no circumstances will arise which would justify a strike on such a scale. But the mere possibility that they may is enough to justify the present retention of the deterrent along with the appropriate war-fighting plans.

A Limited Attack

Such an argument, in my view, is the most powerful form that an ethical defence of the deterrent can take. I shall argue that nonetheless it is inadequate.

It is difficult to decide how far such a limited attack on Warsaw Pact targets would be possible: one would need to know much about the economic geography and military dispositions in the Soviet Union. We do know that no corresponding attack on Great Britain would be possible. In Operation Square Leg, a government simulation of a Soviet attack on this country carried out in October 1981, no bombs were assumed to have fallen on inner London. It was assumed that five targets, such as Heathrow, were hit around the periphery. Nevertheless the consequences, which are described in *London after the Bomb* (Oxford University Press, 1982), include 5m dead in the London area within two months of the attack. Even allowing for the lesser density of the population in many

41

parts of eastern Europe, the result of an attack on military and economic targets in Warsaw Pact countries is likely to be tens of millions dead. And of course many of the targets presented by the Warsaw Pact armed forces, on the hypothesis of an invasion of the West, are in friendly Nato nations.

But suppose even 20m Russians, Poles, Czechs and their allies are killed in such an attack. Is that not better than that the West should succumb to totalitarian domination? Is it not a lesser number of deaths than were thought tolerable in the war against Hitler?

There is something grotesque in the idea that because the allies were justified in going to war against Hitler, any war against a totalitarian enemy is justified if it causes fewer deaths than were lost in Hitler's war. First of all, the great majority of deaths in Hitler's war were caused not by the allies, but by Hitler's armies, Hitler's police and Hitler's gaolers: it is absurd to suggest that because we were justified in going to war against Hitler we would be justified in any future war in causing as many deaths as he did. Secondly, few would now claim that even all the deaths inflicted on the allied side were justified. The lives lost in the bombing of Hamburg, Dresden, Hiroshima and Nagasaki by the western allies, the lives taken by the vengeful Russian troops in their victorious advance westward: these hardly provide a paradigm for the measurement of proportionality in future wars. Can we be certain that the war did more good than harm, in the sense that the world was a better place in 1946 than it was in 1938, or even than it would have been in 1946 had there been no war? Even if we can, that does not mean that we can lump together all the deaths caused in the war and say that the good it did was worth the loss of all those lives.

Even if we waive these difficulties, the comparison with the Second World War leaves out of account the most important thing: that the Third World War would be fought, as the Second was not, against an enemy who is himself armed with nuclear weapons. Even if a damage-plan could be devised which would satisfy the strictest scrutiny in accordance with the principles of non-combatant immunity and proportionality, putting it into action against an enemy prepared and willing to launch massive retaliation would be an act of reckless folly. The criteria for just war-making include, it must be remembered, not only proportionality and non-combatant immunity, but also the hope of victory.

Defenders of the deterrent, faced with this objection, make two responses. First, they say that a victim of aggression cannot necessarily be held responsible for the response of the aggressor to the victim's self-defence: a woman has no absolute duty to submit to rape, for instance, even if she believes that resistance will lead to further violence. Hence, any Russian retaliation to a limited western attack would be their responsibility and not ours. Secondly, we have no reason to assume that western resistance on these lines would inevitably lead to an unlimited counter-attack on our cities. In a nuclear war neither side would want escalation; both would be looking for ways to end the struggle; the Soviets would be no less anxious than the Nato allies not to put the cities of their homelands at further risk.

The first response commits an error opposite to that committed in the value judgment about the death-toll in the Second World War. It is a mistake to lump together all the deaths in a war and regard both sides as equally responsible for them: there is a difference between the lives a nation takes and the lives it loses. But it is an equally distorting error to suggest that a government can entirely escape responsibility for the loss of lives which it brings upon its own side by its attacks on an enemy. The major responsibility for such deaths does, of course, rest on the aggressor who causes them; but responsibility also rests on the side which, foreseeing the possibility of such retaliation, goes ahead with its own attack.

It is correct, as the second response reminds us, that there would be no certainty of a massive Soviet response to a limited western attack: in matters involving human choices and decisions, in times of passion and confusion, there can be no scientific prediction or justified certainty in advance of the outcome. But in order for it to be rational to desist from a course of action, it is not necessary that it should be certain to have a catastrophic result: it is sufficient that catastrophe should be a consequence that is more or less likely. After all, the main reason for saying that it is not certain that the Soviets would opt for massive retaliation is that *they* would fear a western response in kind. But that in turn is uncertain. The mere risk of such a response on our side is supposed to be sufficient to make them, as rational human beings, think twice about launching their attack. But should not the risk of their attack, at the earlier stage, provide an equally strong reason for refraining from the limited attack? Moreover, if the Soviets are deterred from a counter-attack against urban centres, it is because they are afraid of an all-out assault on their population. But this, according to the defender of the deterrent, is something that would be immoral in itself, and the threat of which plays no part in the deterrent strategy.

5 Deterrence Without Use

It seems, then, impossible to defend the view that there can be a use of nuclear weapons sufficiently devastating to underpin the deterrent threat, while sufficiently discriminating to be capable of non-murderous execution. What of those who defend the deterrent while agreeing that no actual use of nuclear weapons is defensible? There are those who are resolved never actually to press the nuclear button, and yet who wish to retain nuclear weapons as a deterrent. This seems to be the policy recommended by the Catholic bishops in the United States, and in Britain by Cardinal Basil Hume: use is forbidden, deterrence is permissible.

The qualified approval given by these authorities to deterrence was no doubt influenced by the statement of Pope John Paul II to the United Nations special session in 1982: "In current conditions, 'deterrence' based on balance, certainly not as an end in itself, but as a step on the way toward a progressive disarmament, may still be judged morally acceptable." The American bishops, in spite of their profound scepticism about the moral acceptability of any use of nuclear weapons, stopped short of an unequivocal condemnation of deterrence, though they rejected any quest for nuclear superiority or plans for prolonged periods of repeated nuclear strikes, and they insisted that deterrence must be a step on the way to disarmament, towards which they recommended a number of specific proposals.

Cardinal Hume, in an article in *The Times* on 17th November

1983, wrote that

> The acceptance of deterrence on strict conditions and as a temporary expedient leading to progressive disarmament is emerging as the most widely accepted view of the Roman Catholic Church.

It would be wrong, the Cardinal said, to apply to the policy of deterrence the same moral condemnation that would be given to the actual use of nuclear weapons against civilian targets, which was something that nothing could ever justify. Since the purpose of deterrence was to avoid war, servicemen could be commended, and not blamed, for taking their part in maintaining it. But the condition that deterrence should be a stage towards disarmament was crucial: a government which failed to reduce its weapons and limit their employment could expect its citizens to be alienated from its defence policies. And finally deterrence had to be seen as a means of preventing, not waging, war: "If it fails and the missiles are launched, then we shall have moved into a new situation. And those concerned will have to bear a heavy responsibility." How they should carry out this responsibility Cardinal Hume did not say. Presumably, whatever they do, they must not use nuclear weapons in the way he has already condemned, "as weapons of massive and indiscriminate slaughter".

The Cardinal admits that his position is a strange one. There is a tension between the moral imperative not to use such inhuman weapons and a policy of nuclear deterrence with its declared willingness to use them if attacked. To condemn all use and yet to accept deterrence places us in a seemingly contradictory position. Many, even among the Catholic Church, are yet to be convinced that if all use is wrong, deterrence is still permissible. Some, convinced of the wrongness of the use of the weapons, deplore the lack of an authoritative and unequivocal condemnation of deterrence. Others, accepting the Pope's judgment that deterrence, as things are, is tolerable, take issue with the American bishops' outspoken "no" to nuclear warfare.

Is the position represented by Cardinal Hume in fact self-contradictory? Would a deterrent operated by people who believed that nuclear weapons must never be used be either credible or ethical? Would there be any point in retaining bombs that one was resolved never to drop and missiles one was determined never to launch?

It can, I think, be argued that such a policy is perfectly consistent with deterrent theory, as well as in accord with the demands of proportionality and non-combatant immunity. The point of deterrence is to provide an input to the practical reasoning of a potential adversary. If an adversary proves to be undeterred, then the deterrent has failed to be effective at the time when it was purported to be effective, and cannot, as it were, be made retrospectively effective by a retaliatory strike. Thus far, then, deterrence without use seems possible.

The difficulty in a deterrent policy of this sort is that if it is announced to the enemy in advance, it is not obvious that the possession of nuclear weapons would continue to deter. The proponents of deterrence normally regard it as essential that the possession of the weapons should be accompanied by the threat, explicit or implicit, to use them if need arise. Those who wish to defend deterrence while opposing use therefore have to be prepared to maintain that it can be legitimate to threaten what it would not be legitimate to do. Is this a defensible ethical position?

It may be argued that the threat to use nuclear weapons cannot be justified, for if it is insincere it involves deception, and if it is not insincere it involves the intention to do what we have agreed it would be wrong to do. This argument moves a little too fast, and it is worthwhile to take it to pieces to see how far it works and how far it does not.

It is difficult to deny the moral principle that if it is wrong to do X, it is wrong to intend to do X. The principle is not an idiosyncrasy of Catholic moral theology. The point has been well put by Barry Paskins in a contribution to *Ethics and Nuclear Deterrence* (Croom Helm, 1982). One cannot argue, he says, that

47

the intention to wage all out nuclear war is less immoral than the action itself:

> If I plan to beat you up and do so, then there is more for me to re-proach myself about than if my plan is thwarted. This indicates one thing that might be meant by holding that the intention to beat you up is "less immoral than" the deed and could be applied to any immoral deed *considered in retrospect*. But retrospection is not the issue. The question is whether looking forward, deliberating what to do, one can in good faith ask whether a conditional intention is as immoral as the act intended. The answer is surely that the question, if clearly evisaged, is bound to be disingenuous. Prohibiting an action sets limits to what may be purposed, selected, intended, done: separate prohibition of intention is otiose.

The intention which Paskins is discussing is, as he says, a conditional one: it is not the intention to launch the missiles, period, but the intention to launch the missiles *if attacked onself*. But this does not affect the argument in this case. It can sometimes be legitimate to intend to do X if A, when it would not be legitimate to intend X *simpliciter*: it is all right to intend to imprison someone *if duly convicted* when it would not be all right to intend to imprison him come what may. But a case where intending to do X if A is legitimate must be a case where actually doing X in circumstances A is legitimate. But if X is some action which is not allowed, whatever the circumstances, then an intention to do X is no more legitimate for being a conditional one.

Moral theologians can be found who are willing to argue that the conditional intention involved in the strategy of deterrence is not an immoral one. Thus, Clifford Longley in *The Times* of 7th February 1983 summarises one argument to this effect, which he attributes to Fr Gerard Hughes:

> I intend to do some immoral action only in certain definite circum-stances. Suppose I also believe that only by having this intention can I be sure that those circumstances will never occur; and suppose that it is my moral duty to try to prevent those circumstances from occurring; the situation then is that only by intending to do an immoral act can I do my duty of preventing those circumstances

from occurring. Is it now clear that that intention is an immoral one?

Hence, Mr Longley suggested, there was a logical fallacy in the arguments of theologians who oppose deterrence. The article drew a reply, two days later, from Bishop B.C. Butler:

> There is certainly a logical fallacy in the above suggestion. For it is impossible to intend to respond to a situation which you are certain will never arise. No one can intend to do what he knows he will never have occasion to do. Hence, if deterrence were certain to succeed permanently, it could continue as a policy, though there would be no intention of translating it into act. Unfortunately, such certainty, as is generally admitted, is not attainable.

This reply seems to be decisive against those who maintain that it is morally acceptable to have a conditional intention to do something which they agree to be morally unacceptable.

The Deterrer's Intentions

It may, however, be questioned whether the maintenance of the deterrent does involve a conditional intention to launch a nuclear attack. The intention of Nato in maintaining a nuclear capability, it is sometimes argued, is not to launch a nuclear attack but to deter a Soviet attack on the alliance. But this argument fails to recognise that the two intentions are not incompatible with each other. The purpose or ultimate intention of maintaining the deterrent is no doubt to dissuade the Soviets and their allies from attacking; but the means chosen of dissuasion is the threat of launching, in the event of an attack, a nuclear counter-attack. Insofar then as the threat involves an intention to attack, that conditional intention is a part of the means to the ultimate purpose of deterrence. The threat is made *in order to* keep the peace, and when X is deliberately done *in order to* bring about Y, X is a means to Y and is something which is itself intentional.

The crucial question is whether the threat to use nuclear weapons if attacked does necessarily involve the conditional intention to use them. The maintenance of the deterrent involves

49

the making of plans for the use of nuclear weapons, the training of servicemen to use them if commanded, the exploration of various consequences of their eventual use. It may well be that the leaders of the West do have, as things are, a quite firm intention to use the weapons in certain specific circumstances, and that these intentions are communicated to the commanders who operate the deterrent in their private briefings. But must a deterrent necessarily involve such intentions? On the part of the supreme policy makers, probably not. For the deterrence to remain effective, the most that is required is that they should not have ruled out the option altogether; that they should, as it were, reserve the right to make a nuclear attack.

It must I think be conceded to defenders of the deterrence strategy that it is misleading for the arguments for and against the morality of the policy to be framed in terms of the intentions of the deterrer. It must be agreed that something less than an intention to use the weapons may be sufficient to deter a potential attacker. A mere willingness to use the weapons will suffice, a willingness which consists in preserving their use as a genuine option.

It is correct to make a distinction between intention and willingness: there can be a great difference between the two states of mind in degree of certainty and resolve implied. But making the distinction does not have a great effect on the course of the moral argument. If it is true that it is wrong to intend to do what it is wrong to do, it is equally true that it is wrong to be willing or ready to do what it is wrong to do. Any argument for the one proposition is an equally good argument for the other. If the wrong in question is an absolute wrong, then it is absolutely wrong to be ready to commit it, just as it is absolutely wrong to intend to commit it. To say that something is absolutely wrong is precisely to say that it is not a permissible option.

To reach a final assessment of the morality of the deterrent we have to ask what exactly it is that does the deterring. As things are the deterrent has two elements. One is the physical element, the nuclear hardware and the power it gives to each side to destroy the other: this is what has been called "the existential deterrent". The other is the political element, the declared intention or readiness of the two sides to use the hardware to destroy the enemy society in certain circumstances. McGeorge Bundy, who introduced the term "existential" into this context, explained his reason as follows:

> My aim in using this fancy adjective is to distinguish this kind of deterrence from the kind that is based on strategic theories or declaratory policies or even international commitments. As long as we assume that each side has very large numbers of thermonuclear weapons which *could* be used against the opponent, even after the strongest possible pre-emptive attack, existential deterrence is strong. It rests on uncertainty about what *could happen*, not in what has been asserted.

Behind each alteration in the strategic plans of the West over recent decades has been a desire to couple the possession of nuclear weapons with a credible threat to use them. Proponents of limited nuclear warfare say that there is a gaping hole in the strategy of MAD: it depends on issuing a threat which the United States could never dare to implement. Critics of the policy of limited war-fighting say that it rests on a premise which hardly anyone in responsibility believes, that nuclear war, once begun, could be kept strictly controlled.

The critics on both sides are right: there is no credible and rational declaratory policy to be enunciated as the justification of nuclear weapons. Even in peacetime, strategists have not been able to present a plan for nuclear weapon use against the Warsaw Pact countries which commands substantial assent among those who would have to carry it out. In wartime any possibility of rational decision would be ruled out by the constraints of timing and the difficulty of maintaining a unified command.

An American president, deciding whether to respond to a Soviet nuclear attack on the mainland of the United States, would have to verify the source of the attack, evaluate the damage it was likely to do, and choose between alternative strategies of defence or retaliation within the 30 minute flight time of an inter-continental missile. In Europe the nuclear weapons which could be used to initiate a nuclear exchange are of many different kinds under many different command structures. Nuclear artillery, battlefield support missiles, and naval weapons are all controlled by different organisations. Army divisions, aircraft carrier groups, fighter squadrons, commando teams and air defence units all have their own nuclear weapons. Theatre nuclear weapons are controlled by seven different command organisations, operating in six different languages, and with no common political goals or structures. Decisions whether or not to respond to Russian attacks would involve identifying whether the attack was nuclear or conventional, since on both sides many of the tactical weapons can be fitted with either kind of warhead. Such choices would have to be made within the ten minutes or so that it takes a Soviet cruise missile such as the Shaddock to reach its target. In such conditions, no pre-ordained unified battle plan could possibly be carried out.

Does the Deterrent Work?

Since no credible plan for the use of our deterrent weapons can be enunciated, it may seem a matter for wonder that the deterrent works at all. Does it, in fact, work? There are two things which can be meant by this question. One is: does it keep the peace? The other is: is it effective in instilling fear? McGeorge Bundy, in the article quoted on page 28, addresses the first question:

> Consider the familiar appeal to history in our current debates over the defence of Europe: "Deterrence has worked for the last 35 years". So it has, if what we mean is that the Soviet Union, barring the quite special case of the blockade of Berlin (which actually preceded the alliance and was lifted shortly after its signing) has never resorted to force in its relations with Nato. But it is only an assumption, and one not open to proof, that the nuclear weapon was indispensable to this result.

Bundy goes on to argue, convincingly, that Russian respect for the freedom of West Berlin since 1971 has not rested on any immediate risk of nuclear war following any interference with it.

But whether or not deterrence works to keep the peace or not, it certainly does work to instil fear. We are each afraid, very much afraid, of the other's deterrent, whether or not this is a rational fear, and whether it is a fear of a rational strategy, or a fear of an enemy's possible suicidal madness. In order to assess the morality of the deterrent, it is important to realise that the fear instilled by it has very little to do with the intentions proclaimed by those who control it. The reason that the possession of nuclear weapons by A works as a deterrent on B is that B *does not know* whether or not A will be mad enough, when the time comes, to launch a nuclear counter-attack. It is a nation's power rather than its willingness to use nuclear weapons that is the essence of the deterrent. And however wicked it may be actually to use nuclear weapons against cities, however wrong it may be to be willing to do so, can the mere possession of a power be something which is immoral in itself?

To answer this question, several points have to be borne in mind. First of all, if our enemies do not know whether we would retaliate by bombing their cities, neither do we. This is so whether "we" means the electorate, the military command, the cabinet or the prime minister. Even the president of the United States does not know what any of his successors would actually do in the event of a Russian attack; he does not know what orders he would himself give in any actual crisis. There exist, of course, many strategic plans worked out in detail, but which of them, if any, is ever put into use no human being can foretell.

The real reason why the way in which we maintain the power to destroy an enemy population is immoral is that in order for the nation to have the power, individuals in the nation must have the willingness to exercise the power. Everyone involved in the military chain of command from the top downwards must be prepared to give or execute the order to massacre millions of non-combatants if ever the government decides that that is what is to be done. It is true that this is a conditional willingness: it is a willingness to massacre if ordered to do so. It is true that it is accompanied, in every member of the armed forces I have ever spoken to, by a profound hope that those orders will never be given. Nonetheless, it is a willingness which is required and insisted upon in all the relevant military personnel.

It is this which is really wrong with the deterrent strategy. To a pacifist, who thinks there should not be armies, navies or air forces at all, it probably seems no great extra iniquity that the military should be trained in readiness to massacre. To someone like myself, who thinks that the military profession is in itself an honourable and indeed noble one, it is very horrible that we should be following a policy which makes it a mark of the good serviceman to be willing, in the appropriate circumstances, to commit murder on a gigantic scale.

Defenders of the deterrent will argue that the conditional willingness to engage in massacre which is an essential element of the policy is a slight and almost metaphysical evil to weigh in the balance against the good of preserving the peace. The moral blemish with which this may taint us in the eyes of the fastidious is at best something to be put on the debit side, along with the financial cost of the weapons systems, against the massive credit of maintaining our independence and our security from nuclear attack. Unilateral disarmament might perhaps make our hands a little cleaner and save us some disagreeable expense; but so far from reducing the risk of war it might actually bring it nearer.

Peacetime Planning Matters

It may seem absurd to concentrate so much attention on the present intentions, attitudes and options of those responsible for the operation of the deterrent. Surely there is a huge gap between mental states of this kind and actual deeds in warfare: is it not infantile idealism to insist so heavily on purity of intention in policy-makers and strategists? After all, even Christians do not seem to take very literally the saying of Jesus that he who lusts after another woman is an adulterer, or St John's teaching that he who hates his brother is a murderer. Surely it is elsewhere that we should be looking for the morally relevant features of our nuclear policies: we should be weighing up the <u>risks of deterrence against the risks of</u> disarmament.

We shall come to weigh up the risks in a moment. But we must first insist that it is not, in this case, unpractical idealism to focus attention on the peacetime attitudes of those in power and those who serve in the armed forces. In an old-fashioned war there was much time for reflection, for changes of mind, for cabinet discussion, for weighing the pros and cons of strategies, for investigating and evaluating alternative options and battle plans. The actual decisions of the British war cabinet in the Second World War were very different from anything that the members of the cabinet would have foreseen or planned before the war. (Not, of course, that the changes of mind were always an improvement from the ethical point of view!) But in the Third World War all will be different: <u>the speed with which decisions will have to be taken will mean that the peacetime attitudes and planning of those involved will play the decisive role.</u>

If a nuclear exchange should ever take place, the key links in the causal chain which will have led up to it will be the options drawn up in peacetime and the pre-war intentions, attitudes and mental inclinations of those who take the eleventh- hour decisions which ignite the holocaust. This fact was well drama-tised in a sequence in the film *The Day After*. The American personnel who have, in a matter of moments, launched the intercontinental ballistic missile for which they are responsible discuss whether they are obliged to remain at their post by the empty silo. They are persuaded to go home and await there the incoming Soviet missiles. "After all," they say, "the war is over now; we have done our duty."

There will, however, one hopes, be a moment for change of heart or last-minute repentance on the part of those who now proclaim that if it comes to the crunch they will launch a nuclear attack rather than surrender. This, indeed, is the key issue at the heart of the ethical debate about deterrence, the question: "<u>What do you do if the deterrent fails?</u>" This is the question which Cardinal Hume declined to answer, but it is the crucial one. In argument with defenders of the deterrent, there always comes a point where one wishes to put this question to one's interlocutor:

> Suppose that deterrence breaks down: suppose, that is, that you are faced with a choice of carrying out the deterrent threat, or of forfeiting the good things which the deterrent was meant to protect. What do you do then? I accept that the whole point of having a deterrent is to prevent being faced with the choice of using it or surrendering; but one can have no certainty that this choice will never have to be faced. Suppose that it fails, and you are faced with the choice: what, in your heart, do you think you should do?

If my friend says that if, God forbid, it ever did come to such a point, then obviously the only thing to do is to surrender—if he says that, then I know that fundamentally we are morally at one, and we can settle down in a comparatively relaxed way to discuss questions of risk and danger and expense. But if he says "Well, I hate to have to say it, but if you are committed to the deterrent, you have to stick to what you believe in and you must go right on and use it if it ever comes to the crunch"—if he says that and means it, then I can only tell him, quite soberly, that he is a man with murder in his heart.

6 The Dangers of Deterrence

Let us now consider the dangers involved in deterrence and in disarmament. If our deterrent policies are based on a fundamental willingness to commit murder, we cannot continue with them unaltered. But anyone who wishes to propose a change must show that he appreciates the dangers involved in alternative policies, and must compare them with the dangers of our present courses. He must be prepared to face and answer the charge that his proposals will make the risks of war increase rather than diminish.

There is also another motive, from the opposite quarter, for an examination of the dangers of deterrence and disarmament. Not all the opponents of our present policies base their opposition on an objection to the threat they present to innocent Warsaw Pact lives: many, perhaps most, of those who demonstrate against Nato nuclear weapons do so because of the dangers which those weapons hold out for the lives of innocent people in our own countries in the West. Some readers, indeed, may have grown impatient that so much of this book has been devoted to showing how the possession of nuclear weapons makes it likely that we will kill people unjustly: is it not time to say something about the likelihood that we will be killed ourselves?

The objection to nuclear weapons on the grounds of their dangerousness is well founded, but it is an argument of a different kind from those considered hitherto. If a policy is murderous, then it ought to be given up, and that is an end of the matter. But if a policy is dangerous, that does not settle by itself whether it should be abandoned. It needs to be shown that it is more dangerous than alternative policies, and that is a more complex and difficult question.

What is it for a course of action to be dangerous? A danger is a likelihood of a bad consequence, so in assessing the extent of danger there are two factors to be considered: the badness of the consequence and the likelihood of its occurrence. In comparing two dangers we have to compare not only the comparative evil of the anticipated outcomes, but the comparative likelihood of their coming to pass.

A defender of the deterrent may well admit that all-out nuclear war is a greater evil than communist domination: not all deterrent theorists believe that it is better to be dead than red in that sense. But though nuclear war is worse than communist domination, it is argued, unilateral disarmament presents a much greater risk of communist domination than the main-tenance of deterrence presents of nuclear war. Suppose, for the sake of argument, that nuclear war is 10 times as bad as communist domination; still, unilateral disarmament makes communist domination virtually certain, while maintenance of the deterrent presents no more than a 1% risk of war. Hence the deterrent policy is 10 times as rational as unilateral abandon-ment of the deterrent.

The Risk of War

Many arguments of this pattern have been presented: the mathematics naturally tends to vary from this simple form, and the particular odds and valuations can be the topic of lengthy argument. Defenders of the deterrent emphasise the enormity of the evil of totalitarian domination, and estimate the Soviet threat to western countries as urgent and substantial. They offer comparatively low estimates of the damage done by a limited first use of nuclear weapons, and of the likelihood of escalation to full-scale war. Their opponents tend to minimise the Soviet threat and emphasise the dangers of escalation. On both sides the arguments take the form of the weighing of two kinds of risk: the risk of nuclear war, and the risk of communist hegemony.

To discuss the matter purely in these terms involves a serious confusion. Talking of the risk of war involves the <u>fallacy of considering war as a self-generating event like a storm or a flood.</u> It takes more than one side to make a war; a nuclear war between the superpowers would be something that the West had to be a party to no less than its enemies. The risk of war is not something which can be assessed without reference to our own future policies and decisions. This may seem a trifling point. No doubt there is a moral distinction between the things we do and the things that are done to us, but to the victims of war it makes little difference who started it. Perhaps our enemies cannot go to war with us without our complicity, but they can certainly attack us without our leave. From the prudential if not from the moral point of view, <u>the risk of nuclear attack is every bit as much to be feared as the risk of a two-sided nuclear war.</u>

However, even the wickedest enemy is unlikely to launch a nuclear attack for no reason. He is <u>likely to do so either in retaliation or to gain some military</u> or political objective. We can avoid an attack of the first kind by renouncing first use of nuclear weapons; and we can avoid an attack of the second kind, if in no other way, by conceding the military or political objective of the enemy before he attacks. No doubt this would be an intolerably humiliating thing to have to do. But let us be clear that <u>humiliating retreat is one of the options open</u>: it is not something ruled out by logic, metaphysics, or morality. We may indeed be grateful that at the moment when the world came closest to nuclear war, during the Cuban missile crisis of 1962, humiliating retreat was the option which was chosen by one of the protagonists, namely the Soviet Union.

The risk that we incur if we disarm is not a risk of nuclear war, nor a risk of nuclear attack: we abolish the first by disarming, and we can avoid the second, if necessary, by surrender. The principal danger that we bring closer if we disarm is not war or nuclear catastrophe: it is the possibility of being forced to surrender by the mere threat of nuclear attack. This is the main danger which has to be weighed against the dangers of our present policies.

In order to weigh up the dangers of deterrence and disarmament it is important to separate in detail the risks which are incurred by both courses. The risks, on both sides, can be classed in six groups: risks which concern future actions on our own part; those which concern Russian nuclear attack; those which concern nuclear strikes by third parties; those concerning what is called "accidental nuclear war"; those which concern conventional attack; and those which can be summed up under the head of nuclear blackmail. The dangers listed towards the end of this catalogue are those specially associated with disarmament, and will be considered in the final section of this book; those listed nearer the beginning are specially associated with deterrence and will be considered now.

A nation which possesses nuclear weapons, or even simply the know-how to produce them, runs the risk that its leaders, in the event of crisis, will use them in a murderous way. This is so whether or not the nation declares its unwillingness to use nuclear weapons; it is so even if a nation actually disarms. But the risk is obviously diminished to the extent that the strategic policy is made less immediately dependent on the more murderous options, and this is something which is favoured by many even among those who would oppose unilateral disarmament.

The risk of murderous use by one's own side is in one way the most important of the risks which advocates of disarmament seek to lessen. But in another way there is something rather odd in talking about this as a risk at all. To describe as a risk what we or those acting in our name might do in a crisis is something which smacks of trying to distance oneself from one's responsibilities. Taking risks about one's own future actions is not in the same category as taking risks about dangers arising from natural causes or the intervention of third parties or acts of God. To treat it as if it were the same kind of thing is a form of bad faith, in the sense which has been explored in detail by writers such as Sartre.

Cases of this kind of thing in private life are not hard to find. Let us suppose that someone is anxious to put an end to an affair *e.g.* which is threatening to wreck his marriage. If, notwithstanding his resolve, he continues to frequent places where he is likely to meet the beloved he wants to give up, his friends are likely to regard his actions not just as imprudent, but as calling in question the sincerity of his desire to save his marriage.

The matter is not so simple in the case of public policies, where governments are acting in the name of their citizens. Moreover an administration which presses a nuclear button may be a different administration from the one which set up the button to press. But the principle remains the same, that a risk about a future decision for which one has a responsibility is a risk different in kind from risks about actions outside one's control. Each succeeding administration must bear in mind not only its own policies but the likely policies of the successors to which it hands on its arsenal; and each citizen, in assessing the dangers of the possession of nuclear weapons by his own country, must remember that in a democracy each succeeding administration acts in the name of the whole citizenry.

The most palpable risk in the possession of a nuclear armoury *2)* is that each nuclear weapon installed in one's own country is one more nuclear target for the nuclear warheads of an adversary. When the British Labour government decided to give the United States Air Force facilities in Britain in 1951, Winston Churchill commented: "We must not forget that by creating the American atomic base in East Anglia, we have made ourselves the target and perhaps the bull's eye of a Soviet attack." In 1979 and 1981 President Brezhnev gave an undertaking that the Soviet Union would not use nuclear weapons against states that did not possess them or station them on their territory. No doubt it would be unwise to rely on the unsupported word of a

Soviet leader, but it would indeed be in the interest of any power not to resort to nuclear attack unless it were regarded as absolutely necessary. A victory which hands over to the victor a country devastated by nuclear war is a hollow victory; and many of the collateral disasters of a nuclear war are likely to fall on aggressor as well as victim. The one thing which really seems to offer a country a motive for nuclear threats and nuclear attacks is the prevention of such attacks and such threats against itself.

It must never be forgotten that nuclear weapons are not just a means of waging war to achieve other goals, such as territory, economic advantage and political domination, but a powerful motivation for war in themselves. The desire to remove the nuclear threat of an adversary provides the most valuable prize to be won by warfare, whether nuclear or conventional, in the nuclear age. It is clear that, rightly or wrongly, many Soviet observers see the deployment in Europe of Pershing-2s, with their 50kt warheads only eight minutes flying time from the outskirts of Moscow, as an enhancement of the threat to the Soviet Union comparable to the increased threat to the United States when the Russians attempted to install missiles in Cuba. The temptation to embark on an enterprise to remove them must be strong: no doubt it is counterbalanced by fear of the strategic deterrent.

Nuclear War by Accident

Many people regard one of the greatest risks attendant on the possession of nuclear weapons as that of nuclear war occurring by accident. Strictly speaking, it is not possible for war to be made by accident: it must involve human decision. There is a risk, and a horrible one, of a nuclear explosion occurring by accident: a nuclear warhead may explode as a result of human negligence. There is also a risk that due to the malfunction of information gathering or processing systems, decision-makers in the governments of superpowers may launch attacks on the basis of faulty data. In 1979 a mistake by an operator in the

North American Aerospace Defence Command (Norad) head-quarters near Colorado Springs led to the transmission of an erroneous message that the United States was under nuclear attack. Fighters were scrambled and sent airborne from three separate bases, and missile and submarine bases switched to a higher level of alert. Several months later a similar message, which led to 100 B-52 bombers being readied for take-off, was the result of a failed chip in a mini-computer. In each case the error was discovered before harm was done. Full nuclear war cannot be launched except by the decisions of human beings, whether in the East or the West or elsewhere.

Nonetheless, there is a danger that the structure of military organisations, and the tight linkage which now exists between information-gathering and attack-launching systems on both sides, may lead to the outbreak of a nuclear war which nobody on either side really wants. The seriousness of this danger has been soberly documented in Paul Bracken's chilling study *The Command and Control of Nuclear Forces* (Yale University Press, 1983).

The danger, according to Bracken, arises from three factors: the vulnerability of the communications systems on both sides; the predelegation of powers from the supreme commands to local commanders; and the strategies of decapitation strikes.

The central American Norad headquarters in Colorado Springs has been hardened against attack, but competent judges doubt whether it is invulnerable: the Soviet Union probably has missiles of sufficient power and accuracy to destroy it. But even if it survives, it is dependent on a constant flow of information from satellites and elsewhere, which is processed in other sites presenting a soft target for an early attack. Without this, it will be impossible to make decisions with knowledge of what attacks have been made or are pending, what damage has been done, what forces remain on each side. Even if decisions can be taken, it is necessary for the communications system to continue to function if they are to be communicated to commanders in the field. How can the supreme command direct the war if it cannot keep in touch with the men actually launching strikes on the enemy? And how can war be limited if it cannot be directed? As nuclear strategies have become more complicated, the ability to carry out these strategies has been declining. The more complicated the strategy, the more elaborate the system of command and control which is necessary. No adequate system has been built, because no one has any idea how to build it.

Instead, an elaborate system of predelegation of powers appears to be in force. The president and the joint chiefs of staff constitute a National Command Authority (NCA). As one NCA is destroyed, it is replaced by another, and that in turn by another. If subordinate commanders are unable to communicate with the current NCA, they are in wartime circumstances authorised to release nuclear weapons on their own authority. As each link to headquarters is broken, individual commanders, down to bomber pilots and submarine captains, have predelegated authority to proceed. The purpose of this is to prevent a Soviet attack on the supreme command or the communications system from immobilising the American strategic force. The disadvantage of it is that it would make a nuclear war almost impossible to bring to an end. A Soviet Union which wished to surrender after the NCA had been cut off from its communications network might have to negotiate a ceasefire with each of the five separate commands immediately subordinate to it. In peacetime, of course, there is no predelegated authority to fire if communication is interrupted, but the war system, in the Pentagon jargon, is programmed to "fail safe" in peacetime, and to "fail deadly" in war. Low-level nuclear initiative on the American side would lead to semi-automatic response from the Soviet side. Such exchanges would lead to a total collapse of communications, leaving all surviving nuclear units authorised to use their weapons at their own discretion.

American difficulties in controlling a nuclear war would be matched by equal difficulties on the Soviet side. This makes it almost incredible that American strategy since PD-59 has called for early strikes on the enemy's command and control structure. Such a declaratory strategy is highly dangerous in two ways. First, it is likely to lead to the adoption by the Soviet Union of dangerous policies such as launch-under-attack plans. Second, it means that at the beginning of a war, the United States would be cutting off all possibility of bringing it to an end. To "terminate the war on advantageous terms" you need to have someone left to negotiate with. The danger facing the world, Bracken maintains, is that the superpowers may have institutionalised a major nuclear showdown. They have built the most complex technological apparatus ever conceived, without devising any method of controlling it. Because of the instabilities of the command structures of the superpowers, it is a real possibility that 200m people may be killed for no purpose at all.

Bracken's ultimate warning is more alarming still:

> Instead of asking whether nuclear *war* can be controlled, it is more important to ask whether nuclear *alerts* can be controlled. If forces cannot be safely put on alert without the alert process becoming so provocative and dangerous that the alert order is tantamount to a declaration of war, then two dangers follow. First, alerts may directly lead to war, through accident or inadvertence—or through compelling an opponent to pre-empt merely to protect himself. A full dispersal and alerting of theatre nuclear weapons in Europe would surely force the Soviets to think about this. Second, the dangers of alerting may be so apparent as to paralyse political leaders into taking no action whatsoever. Here, virtually all room for manoeuvre would be removed and political leaders, especially in Europe, would be faced with a decision of being either "red or dead".

Pascal's Wager

It has been well said that the way to decide about the risks of deterrence and disarmament is to apply the kind of reasoning put forward by Pascal in his celebrated wager argument. Pascal maintained that we ought to believe in God because the penalties for not believing in him if he existed amounted to infinite loss, while the penalty for believing in him if he did not exist was merely a degree of modest but unnecessary self-discipline. Similarly, the worst case outcome of deterrence, namely nuclear devastation, is so much more catastrophic than the worst case outcome of disarmament, Russian domination, that the course which leads to it should be avoided no matter what the relative probabilities of the two outcomes of the different strategies.

Pascal's wager is not successful as a motive for believing in God because it involves a flight from the pursuit of truth on a matter where, on Pascal's own principles, it was a matter of enormous consequence that one should be guided by the truth. But in adopting a policy concerning nuclear weapons we are not anxious to attain metaphysical truth nor to predict the future of the universe: we are looking for a strategy to minimise danger under conditions of high uncertainty. Pascal's hell was a literally infinite loss; nuclear devastation cannot claim to be infinite in the same sense. But the Pascalian policy is appropriate wherever the evils in the worst case outcome are incommensurable in scale, and the havoc of the aftermath of nuclear war is indeed an evil disproportionate to any political goal to be achieved by the possession of the deterrent.

Even if we attempt, then, to base our nuclear strategy on the calculation of risk, the policy of deterrence seems to be objectionable. In the next section we will consider the risks involved in alternative policies, for those too are undeniably great. But once again it must be said that attempts to base nuclear policy on the calculation of risk alone leave out of account the most important moral point. This is the principle, basic to European morality since its enunciation by Socrates, that it is better to undergo wrong than to do wrong. The principle holds good even when the evils in question are, considered in isolation from the question of who perpetrates them, comparable in scale. But of course the evil we would do if we used nuclear weapons in a major war would be incomparably greater than the evil we would suffer if the worst came to the worst after nuclear disarmament.

III. THE REALITIES OF DISARMAMENT

7 Unilateral or Multilateral?

Almost everyone, nowadays, professes to be in favour of disarmament. It seems to be generally agreed that the existing stockpiles of the superpowers go beyond anything which could be rationally or ethically justified. But despite repeated statements of the urgency of disarmament, not only in the United Nations but also by the leaders of the nuclear powers, there has been notoriously little progress towards that goal.

On the basis of what has been said in the previous chapters, the arsenal of the West is objectionable on three grounds: that much of it can only be used, in practice, in ways that are murderous; that much of it is superfluous in the sense that it goes beyond the strategic and political purposes it is supposed to serve, leaving aside any moral evaluation of those purposes; and that much of it increases the risk of nuclear attack by providing extra targets likely to attract the attention of a potential aggressor. But what conclusions in practice should be drawn from the ethical objections to the nuclear arsenal? If the argument hitherto has been sound, then the deterrent policy which the nuclear weapons now serve is a morally unacceptable policy based upon a willingness to kill millions of innocent people. It seems clear, then, that this policy must be given up, and that if the weapons are to be retained at all it must be for some totally different purpose. But can we justify the retention of the weapons if we give up the deterrent policy, or must we immediately and unilaterally disarm?

Different opinions are strongly held here even among those

who agree in condemning the present policy. Barry Paskins, who maintains that the Soviet and western deterrents are immoral no less than nuclear war, offers one answer to the question:

> So what is to be done? Even in private life it is not always right to stop doing something at once on recognising its immorality. An example may make this plain. Consider a man conducting two adulterous affairs who comes to recognise that each of the two affairs is immoral. Suppose one affair can be ended coolly with little hurt—Thanks for the Memory—whereas the other mistress is suicidally dependent on the relationship. Plainly, it would be as wrong to terminate the latter affair at once as it would be to continue the former. The ending of our conditional intention to wage all-out nuclear war seems to involve the complexities of the more difficult of the two liaisons, not least because there are no God-given rules of disengagement.

He argues, therefore, for deep unilateral cuts in the West's deterrent, but not for complete disarmament.

Other Christian voices have expressed the conviction that the chances of nuclear weapons ever serving purposes other than evil ones are so slender that they must be immediately and unconditionally dismantled. They commend unilateral disarmament not as a policy of prudence but as a moral imperative. The dangerous consequences of disarmament are the price we must pay for giving up our past evil courses. We must keep God's law and trust in God's mercy: our future is in His hands, and they are good hands.

Most people, even among Christians opposed to nuclear war, hesitate at the prospect of complete unilateral nuclear disarmament by the West. Even a motion calling for the United Kingdom to declare its intention of carrying out "a phased disengagement from active association with any form of nuclear weaponry" was defeated at the General Synod of the Church of England in February 1983. And the American Catholic bishops contented themselves with saying, on the topic of unilateral disarmament:

> Arms control and disarmament must be a process of verifiable agree-

ments especially between two superpowers. While we do not advocate a policy of unilateral disarmament, we believe the urgent need for control of the arms race requires a willingness for each side to take some first steps.

But of course both the American bishops and the majority in the General Synod are supporters of the deterrent in spite of their opposition to nuclear war. What judgment should an opponent of the deterrent make about unilateral disarmament?

A False Dichotomy

The first thing to be said is that it is misleading to draw a simple contrast between unilateralism and multilateralism. It is wrong to divide the world into unilateralist disarmers and multilateralist disarmers, and to put to everyone the pollster's alternative: "Are you a unilateralist or a multilateralist?"

First of all, we must distinguish between unilateralism as a goal and unilateralism as a means. No serious unilateralist has unilateral disarmament as a goal: that is to say, no serious unilateralist sees, as an ideal to be aimed for, a situation in which one side is totally disarmed of nuclear weapons while the other retains them. No doubt there are some in the American military establishment who would like to see the Soviet Union totally disarmed, and some in the Soviet military establishment who would like to see the United States totally disarmed. If there are Russian agents in the Campaign for Nuclear Disarmament (CND), no doubt they support its aims because they would like to see the West disarmed while Russia retains its arsenal. But genuine members of such organisations regard unilateralism not as an end but as a means. They regard unilateral steps as the only way to bring about, so far as is possible, multilateral disarmament, or if that is not possible, at least the security that governments which act in our name will not launch into nuclear massacre.

On the other hand, many multilateralists are not really in favour of disarmament at all. By calling themselves multilateralists they merely mean that they are not unilateralists:

they may in fact favour arms control, or the maintenance of the present defence systems, or an actual increase in armaments designed to secure a balance of power. None of these three courses need involve any actual reduction of arms, but for some reason it is fashionable to pretend that we are all disarmers now.

Instead, therefore, of labelling oneself a unilateralist or a multilateralist it is more helpful to spell out in detail what policies one believes should replace the present reliance on the nuclear deterrent.

On the basis of the arguments of the previous chapters, it appears that the following course would avoid the moral objections to our present policies, while preserving an adequate defence for the western allies, and would hold out a realistic prospect of the reduction and eventual elimination of nuclear weapons throughout the world.

A Unilateralist Agenda

(1) The West should immediately unilaterally and credibly renounce the actual use of nuclear weapons. It should renounce not only first use on the battlefield but also second use in retaliation, whether against cities or military targets in populated areas.

(2) Projected future nuclear weapons systems should be cancelled, and an immediate nuclear freeze established unilaterally by the West. Every diplomatic effort should be made to turn this into a multilateral freeze.

(3) Existing nuclear weapons systems should be dismantled in an orderly fashion and in such a way as to secure reciprocating arms reductions by the Warsaw Pact powers. The process should begin with the withdrawal of intermediate range weapons such as the Tomahawk cruise missiles and the Pershing-2 missiles recently installed in Britain and West Germany. Theatre and battlefield nuclear weapons should be gradually removed from the European landmass. The independent strategic deterrents of Britain and France should be wound down. The airborne and landlaunched components of the

American nuclear strategic triad should be phased out.

(4) Simultaneously with the removal of theatre nuclear weapons from the European theatre, the conventional defences of the central front should be strengthened. But they should be strengthened in a way that is unambiguously defensive and cannot be construed as any threat of aggression against the Soviet Union. Every effort should be made to exploit the advantage which the development of recent technology has given to the defence over the offence in conventional warfare.

(5) During these steps of disarmament, and until Soviet response to these steps presents a realistic hope of complete nuclear disarmament on both sides, the submarine-based strategic nuclear force of the western deterrent should not be completely dismantled.

The individual items of this programme and the order in which it is proposed that it should be carried out need detailed justification which they will receive later. But the general concept of such phased and partial unilateral disarmament needs immediate defence against criticism from two sides. On the one hand, anti-unilateralists will say that the degree of unilateral disarmament proposed in the first three items is intolerably dangerous. On the other, unilateralists who call for the immediate dismantling of all western nuclear weapons will say that the retention, even as a bargaining counter, of submarine-based nuclear warheads renders the proposed policy liable to all the moral objections to deterrence which I have expounded in the previous section of the book. I will reply to these two objections in turn.

Unilateral steps of disarmament are described by their opponents as being "destabilising". The word suggests that any unilateral steps will upset the fragile vessel of peace in which we voyage on the dark dangerous waters of a nuclear world. But the metaphor of destabilisation really depends on the metaphor of balance. Peace, we are told, depends on a balance of power between the giants of East and West: to upset that balance is to endanger peace. "Balance" is then interpreted as a roughly equal number of warheads, or missiles, or yield, or throw-weight on each side. Any unilateral proposal which means that our side, even temporarily, has less than rough parity with the other side in terms of the preferred method of calculation is therefore destabilising and must be resisted by true friends of peace. (Unilateral reduction by the other side is not regarded as destabilising in the same way, though in terms of the metaphor of the balance it should be. Perhaps that ought to suggest that there is something suspicious about the metaphor.)

If it is true that peace is kept by a balance of power, it is kept because each side has the power to destroy the other. In fact, it is well known that each side has the power to destroy the other several times over: it is not necessary, in order to keep the peace, that each side should have that power exactly as many times over as the other side has. Still less is it necessary that each side should match the other in each possible measure of comparison between weapons, or in each element of the strategic triad of land-, sea- and air-launched missiles. Even according to the logic of deterrence, then, unilateral steps need not be destabilising in the sense of dangerous. It could, no doubt, be dangerous to pass from our present condition into a state in which one side felt that it could destroy the other with impunity—whether this was reached by the total unilateral disarmament of one side, or by the other's believing that it had obtained a first-strike capability of knocking out the other. But the five proposals outlined above do not provide for the bringing about of such a state of affairs. While a strategic submarine force remains in existence the West retains the power to destroy the Soviet Union; and of all forms of launching platforms for nuclear weapons, submarines are the least vulnerable to any kind of first-strike.

It remains true, however, that on the principles outlined in earlier chapters, the West would never be justified in making warlike use of the nuclear ballistic missiles retained as a bargaining counter. If, in the course of the programme I have proposed, there came to a point where western leaders believed that they were faced with a choice between giving in to a Soviet demand and actually using the power of nuclear devastation they had retained, they would have to choose to give in. The steps of the programme have been chosen to make it unlikely that such a choice would ever arise, but the remote possibility of its arising must be faced. So the dangers involved in this modified unilateralism must now be evaluated. They fall, as said earlier, into several classes: dangers of Soviet nuclear attack, danger of nuclear war between third parties, danger of Soviet conventional attack and dangers of nuclear blackmail.

8 The Dangers of Disarmament

It was argued earlier that the removal of nuclear bases from the European landmass and from the American homeland would make Russian nuclear attack less likely by removing the prime targets of such an attack. But it is argued on the other side that to the extent that a country deprives itself of nuclear weapons, it makes it more and not less likely that it will be the victim of an attack by an enemy who retains them. Is it not hard to believe that the Americans would have dropped atomic bombs on Japan in 1945 if the Japanese had themselves had a nuclear capacity?

The answer to the question of whether nuclear disarmament makes nuclear attack more or less likely must be given by making a distinction. The removal of nuclear weapons surely makes a peacetime nuclear attack less and not more likely. The only credible scenario in which the Soviet Union would use nuclear weapons to attack a western nation in peacetime would be in order, by a pre-emptive strike, to destroy that nation's own capability of attacking the Soviets. If the nation voluntarily foregoes that capability, it removes the incentive for the Soviet nuclear strike.

Once a war has started between a nuclear and a non-nuclear power, the matter is altered. If a conventional war is going badly for the nuclear power, it may be tempted to use its power in order to right the balance. This is, after all, what Nato says it intends to do in the event of a conventional war in Europe, though fortunately the United States resisted the temptation to act in this way during the actual wars in Korea and Vietnam. Even if things are going well, a nuclear power may decide, as the United States did in 1945, that a nuclear attack is an acceptable way of shortening the road to complete victory.

But it is wrong to draw the lesson from Hiroshima and Nagasaki that a non-nuclear power is always in greater danger than a nuclear power of being subject to nuclear attack. On the contrary, the reason why nuclear weapons were developed by the United States in the first place was that Germany was believed to be on the threshold of becoming a nuclear power. The Truman administration had no qualms about using nuclear weapons against a non-nuclear power; but a more circumspect administration with qualms about devastating the cities of an empire that was on the verge of surrender might have felt no compunction about using the first two atom bombs on nuclear installations in Japan, if there had been any. And as we said earlier, a warring nation, faced with the prospect of nuclear devastation, always has the alternative of surrender. Had the Japanese been willing to surrender unconditionally in August 1945, as they were willing to surrender conditionally, the bomb would not have been dropped.

Nonetheless, it may well be true that a non-nuclear power at war with a nuclear-armed Soviet Union is more likely to be the subject of a nuclear attack than is a country which itself possesses nuclear weapons. If so, we must conclude that it would be most unwise for a country that has disarmed itself of nuclear weapons to get involved in a war with the Soviet Union. But this is hardly a strong argument against disarmament. It is not as if we were at present in a position from which we can go to war with the Soviet Union with a song in our hearts and our heads held high. We would not, by nuclear disarmament, be giving up some option which we now have of rationally taking on the Russians in a conventional conflict.

Since 1949 there have been a number of occasions on which it might be claimed that there would have been a just cause of war against the Soviet Union. In a non-nuclear world it might have been reasonable to undertake a limited military action in defence of the Hungarians in 1956 or the Czechs in 1968. But as things were the West prudently decided against intervening. Whichever of the other conditions of the just war may have been present, one was absent: good hope of victory.

We are often reminded by defenders of the *status quo* that even if it is true that disarmament reduces the risk of nuclear devastation by Soviet attack, there will always remain the possibility of nuclear war between third parties. Whether or not this involves ourselves directly, it is surely something that we have a duty to prevent as far as we can. Hence, if keeping our deterrent will help prevent such a war, we have a duty to keep it.

Those who argue in this way must regard nuclear weapons in our hands as being fundamentally different from the same weapons in anyone else's hands. We encourage other nations to sign non-proliferation treaties, on the grounds that the more countries who possess nuclear weapons, the greater the risk of nuclear war. But by a unique favour of providence, it seems, our own nuclear weapons have exactly the opposite quality. Alone among the actual and potential weapons systems of the world, they actually decrease the risk of war.

Whatever may be the risks of being a non-nuclear power in a world of nuclear superpowers, they are risks which it is difficult for a country like Britain to avoid with decency. We constantly exhort every other nation to take these risks, by remaining non-nuclear in the interests of non-proliferation. How then can we consistently refuse to run those risks ourselves?

Since we do not wish to retain the option of ourselves making an aggressive war with conventional weapons, I turn to the risk of a conventional attack upon us by an enemy. This is a genuine risk, and it is one which may be increased by nuclear disarmament if that is carried out without a simultaneous strengthening of conventional defences, and a strengthening which can be clearly seen to be non-provocative and purely defensive. It is fortunate that recent developments in military technology make the present juncture a particularly favourable one for such a step.

There remains to be considered the most serious risk of all: the risk of nuclear blackmail. There is no denying that total unilateral disarmament by the western powers would leave them vulnerable to Soviet nuclear blackmail if the Soviet Union retains its nuclear arsenal. And there is no doubt that for a non-nuclear power blackmailed by a nuclear power the only certain way of avoiding nuclear devastation is surrender.

Nuclear Blackmail

Many people, with Churchill's "we shall never surrender" echoing in their ears, will say that the West should never surrender to the Russians, come what may. They will say that we should defend our values and our freedoms, if we believe in them, no matter what the cost. It is hard to know how seriously such remarks are meant, or how carefully they have been thought out. But to take the second first, it is clear that it would be pointless to defend one's values whatever the cost, if that included the forfeiture of those values—as an all-out nuclear exchange would do. And if "surrender" means to lay down one's arms, to give notice that one does not intend to continue defence by force of arms, then it is not only unilateralists who believe that there may come a point at which the only honourable thing is to surrender. Anyone who stops short of the view that we should go on using nuclear weapons as long as it is in our power to do so, must believe that there is a point at which surrender is a more rational option than continuing to fight. Those who have no moral inhibitions about the use of nuclear weapons to destroy an enemy society may perhaps genuinely believe that once war starts the right thing is to go to the limit of one's power to harm or until one is oneself eliminated. But those who think we should not use nuclear weapons to kill populations cannot think this. At each point of military escalation, through conventional and nuclear rungs of the ladder, a combatant who is losing is faced with the choice of escalating or surrendering. Anyone who opposes the destruction of cities must believe that if it comes to the point where the only way to avoid losing a tactical nuclear war is to escalate to countervalue targets, then surrender is the correct option. The unilateralist differs only in thinking that the point to surrender is if it becomes clear that further resistance by conventional weapons will be met by nuclear attack.

How great, in fact, is the danger of blackmail if we disarm? The likelihood of a Soviet resort to such blackmail cannot be scientifically quantified: but no unilateralist should deny that it is a possibility which should be seriously considered. The risk of blackmail is a terrible one but it is a less terrible one than that of nuclear war. For our nations to be reduced to the status of, say, Rumania would be an incomparably lesser disaster than for our cities to be reduced to the condition of Hiroshima and Nagasaki in 1945. We are often told that unilateral disarmament by the West would lead to the "Finlandisation" of western Europe. Those who say this do not always realise how impudent is the judgment that we should be prepared to kill millions rather than accept the political arrangements of Finland. The internal freedoms enjoyed by the Finns compare with the human rights record of any country in the whole world. A Czech friend of mine once remarked to me that if her compatriots were told their country was to be Finlandised they would jump for joy.

But it is in order to minimise the risk of nuclear blackmail, and to maximise the chances of winning reciprocal Soviet arms reductions, that the programme I have suggested envisages the retention of the submarine-based nuclear warheads during the early stages of unilateral disarmament. It is this suggestion which needs defence against the criticism that it is merely a modified form of the present deterrent policy, or a return to the strategy of mutual assured destruction.

It was pointed out earlier that the existing nuclear deterrent has two elements: the operational hardware, which we called the existential deterrent, and the strategy of threats which it subserves, which we called the political deterrent. In assessing the morality of retaining some of the hardware in operation, we have to ask whether the political and the existential element of the deterrent can be separated from each other.

It was observed in the previous section that the possession of nuclear weapons works as a deterrent for reasons which have little to do with the stated policy of the deterrer. A is deterred by B's nuclear weapons because he does not know, when the time comes, whether B will launch a nuclear counter-attack. As things are, each side has good reason to believe that the other is not only able but willing to use the weapons if it comes to the crunch. But the deterrent effect would not disappear, even if B renounced the willingness to use the weapons, as long as he retained the capability of counter-attack. It is a nation's power, rather than its willingness, to use nuclear weapons which gives a potential adversary pause.

Striking a Nuclear Bargain

Now if it could be severed from the willingness to destroy an enemy population, would the mere maintenance of the power to do so necessarily be wrong? That must depend, in part, on how the power is maintained. As things are, everyone involved in the military chain of command, from the top downwards, has to be prepared to give or execute the order to launch nuclear warheads on non-combatants if ever the government decides that this is what is to be done. But must it necessarily be so, and is the only alternative total unilateral disarmament? Suppose that the western powers announced a decision of policy that nuclear weapons were never to be used on cities or military targets near centres of population. Suppose that this decision was a serious, carefully thought out one, prepared for and announced in such a way as to be credible. Suppose that all who were trained in the operation of nuclear weapons systems were given standing orders never to accept commands from anyone to employ them on unacceptable or unknown targets. Might it not then be possible, without incurring the guilt of our present unacceptable policies, to retain sufficient nuclear hardware to enforce the best disarmament bargain that we can with the Warsaw Pact powers?

Objections to the temporary retention of the existential deterrent will be either that such a policy is impossible to execute, or that it is immoral to propose. The argument that the policy is impossible goes like this. A nuclear armoury is not simply an inventory of inert hardware. It requires the activity of many thousands of people involved in training, exercising, operational planning. Those involved in keeping the existential deterrent in the condition of readiness which it would have to preserve if it were to serve any bargaining purpose, would have to be constantly rehearsing actions which they would be expressly prohibited from ever carrying out in earnest. It would be hard to find people willing to devote their lives to such a schizophrenic task. Moreover, to the extent that the official renunciation of the willingness to use the weapons in war is made credible, the credibility of the existential deterrent diminishes to an exactly corresponding extent. Its credibility, and therefore its value as a bargaining counter, would decline in direct proportion to the sincerity and credibility of the no-use declaration which is the essential element in the abandonment of the immoral political deterrent.

This objection can be answered. Those who operate the present deterrent already carry through their exercises with the profound hope that they will never enact what they have rehearsed. They are willing to do so because they believe it helps to preserve peace and freedom. If that which servicemen now have as their hope is turned into the declared policy of their government, why should that depress their morale? Why should they not continue to rehearse what they may never enact in order to further the disarmament of our potential enemies?

The American Secretary of Defense, Mr Caspar Weinberger, stated in his annual report to Congress in 1983: "The Reagan administration's policy is that under no circumstances may [nuclear] weapons be used deliberately for the purpose of destroying populations." This statement did not have any adverse effect on the morale of those entrusted with the operation of the deterrent. Many authorities, from former secretaries of defense to bishops, have called for a sincere declaration of no first use of nuclear weapons. No one has suggested that such a renunciation would be incompatible with continuing to train servicemen in the use of such weapons. If both first use and second use against populations are ruled out, then we are already close to the policy here recommended. But those who rule out such uses clearly consider that such a renunciation is compatible with the retention of a deterrent, and with the training of personnel in readiness to operate it. Why then should not a total renunciation of use be compatible with the retention of the minimum transitional existential deterrent?

It is no new thing to train public servants in the use of lethal force which they will never or rarely have a legitimate occasion to exercise. In Britain we train policemen in marksmanship while aware that the great majority even of those who were armed will never be authorised to use their weapons in anger. Nor is it a new thing for training manuals to include instruction about the type of commands from superior officers which the subordinate is bound to disobey. Commands to kill prisoners or commands which can be interpreted as forms of sexual harassment are already explicitly listed among commands which must not be obeyed. Why should there not be added to the list commands for the launch of nuclear weapons in ways which would violate the laws of war?

An End to Threats

But could the renunciation of the use of nuclear weapons be genuine and credible enough to avoid the moral objections to the deterrent threat, while providing a sufficient motivation to our potential enemies to desist from attack and seek disarmament? The renunciation must indeed be made credible if it is to bring an end to the spiral of threat and counter-threat which constitutes the arms race. No mere verbal declaration will be powerful enough to do this. But if the declaration is accompanied with the change in the programme of training, exercising and planning which has been described, this will quickly be known

81

to our adversaries and will reinforce the credibility of the renunciation as a genuine present intention. The new policy will not, of course, guarantee, and in a democratic state cannot guarantee, that there will be no future reversal of policy and resumption of the threat of nuclear devastation. This will both sober any thoughts of military adventures and give an incentive to multilateral disarmament agreements.

The policy proposed would turn to good purpose a feature of human nature which at present is one of the main fuels of the arms race. We judge our own future actions by our own present intentions; we judge our enemy's future actions not by their present statements but by their present capacities. We regard our own nuclear arsenal as benign because we are confident in the purity of our defensive intentions; we deduce the intentions of our enemies from the capacities which they acquire. Hence, during a period when armaments are mounting, each side regards their own increase in capacity as purely defensive, and the enemy's increase in capacity as manifestly aggressive. In the reduction of nuclear armaments proposed here, we would have better reason to trust in the genuineness of our benign intentions, since they would be backed by concrete steps of disarmament; but our potential enemies would still be dissuaded from rash courses by their tendency to play safe, imputing deterrent intentions from our nuclear capacities.

But if theoretically possible, would such a policy really avoid the moral objections to our present policies? Here we have to meet the second wave of criticism, from the opposite point of the compass. Surely there would be a risk that even if there is an official policy of renouncing the use of nuclear weapons, it may be insincere, and even if it is serious, it may be reversed by later governments. The risk is a genuine one, to be weighed against other risks, and the danger of bad faith is indeed very difficult to guard against. But it is merely the risk that our governments will do secretly or later what they now do explicitly and cheerfully. It is a strategy which avoids the fundamental moral objection to our present policies: it does not call for current plans for murder, nor does it demand a readiness for massacre from the servicemen involved in its maintenance.

It is sometimes objected that a policy such as this would be one of bluff. Bluff must be rejected, it is claimed, because it involves lying, which is morally wrong. Moreover, a policy involving bluff could never succeed: it would depend on preserving a secret which could never be kept. If it were possible to maintain it, a policy of lying threats would be preferable to our present policies. Lying no doubt is wrong, but the wrongness of lying is much less than the wrongness of the willingness to commit mass murder. However it is true that if our threats were lies, and there was no genuine willingness ever to carry them out, this is not a secret which could be preserved. It would have to be kept not only from our enemies, but from our own armed forces and population. <u>One cannot deceive an enemy about one's intentions without deceiving one's friends as well.</u>

But the proposal made above does not involve any element of bluff. Bluff does involve an intention to deceive (whether by lying, as in the simplest case of bluff, or by more sophisticated means, as in double bluff). But here there is no intention to deceive the enemy. He is not meant, as part of the plan, to believe that we will use our nuclear weapons when we say we will not. At most, he may be left in some uncertainty about this. The renunciation of the use of nuclear weapons is publicly announced, and the declaration of renunciation is sincerely meant. If it did indeed involve bluff, this would not be an overwhelming objection against it: military bluffs (for instance, the feint invasion plans before D-Day) have always been regarded, even by quite austere moralists, as legitimate strategy and need not involve any actual lying. But bluff is the wrong word to describe a policy which is aimed at the elimination of nuclear weapons, which announces the renunciation of the use of one's own nuclear weapons, and which takes concrete steps to reinforce and make credible this declaration of renunciation.

I conclude therefore that there is nothing inherently impracticable or inherently immoral in the phased unilateral disarmament I have outlined. Of course the concrete steps in which I have embodied the policy cannot claim to be more than a provisional sketch of a possible scenario. No proposals for unilateral disarmament have yet benefited from more than a fraction of the careful and expensive contingency planning which defence departments have devoted to warfighting and deterrence, neither have they benefited from the dialectical discipline which has been undergone by proposals for multi-lateral disarmament. It may be, though I doubt it, that careful and unbiased consideration of the concept of a minimum transitional existential deterrent would show that it could not serve as a bargaining counter without falling foul of the moral objections to our existing policies. If that proved to be so, then I for my part would give up the possiblity of preserving the deterrent hardware, rather than resign myself to a continuation of the policy of defending ourselves at the cost of murderous threats. In the meantime, all that is claimed is that the proposal should be taken seriously.

9 Defence Without Deterrence

In the previous chapter I outlined a programme of steps towards disarmament, some unilateral and some multilateral. It now remains to explain and justify in greater detail the philosophy behind the proposals.

The most recent round of negotiations between the United States and the Soviet Union in Geneva are aimed in particular at stopping the arms race spreading into space. The joint communique announcing the talks, which began in February 1985, stated: "The sides believe that ultimately the forthcoming negotiations, like efforts in general to limit and reduce arms, should lead to the complete elimination of nuclear arms everywhere."

The history of previous multilateral negotiations, however, does not induce optimism about the likelihood of success. The Strategic Arms Limitations Talks of the 1970s achieved one significant agreement, the Salt I treaty on the limitation of anti-ballistic missile systems (ABMs). The Salt II treaty which was signed in Vienna in 1979 called for a limitation on strategic offensive arms, setting a ceiling on the number of warheads and launchers which the two superpowers were permitted to deploy. Because of the Soviet invasion of Afghanistan this treaty was never ratified by the United States. In practice, however, both sides seem to have kept within the limits set by the treaty. But when President Reagan came to power in 1981 he was unenthusiastic about arms limitation, believing that it had worked to the United States' disadvantage. However, in 1982 he agreed to a new set of talks to replace the abandoned Salt talks. These were designed to lead to a treaty which would not only limit but actually reduce strategic nuclear weapons. Hence they were called Strategic Arms Reduction Talks (Start). But the American proposals seemed more designed to improve their own strategic position than to achieve agreement. Initially, the proposals involved a near 50% cut in ballistic missiles, with a reduction to 5,000 warheads on each side, with no more than 2,500 based on land. This would have involved a drastic cut in Soviet land-based forces (75% of Soviet ballistic missiles were on land) while leaving the United States free to develop its technical superiority in submarine-based missiles. More realistic were the "build-down" proposals of October 1983, whereby the number of missiles would have been reduced to 5,000 by the process of removing more than one warhead for each warhead newly deployed, while leaving each side with flexible choices in the mix of launchers. But the talks were suspended in December 1983 after making very little headway.

Talking INF

Meanwhile, another set of arms control negotiations concerned intermediate range nuclear forces (INF), with the intention of limiting medium-range nuclear missiles in Europe. The principal aim of the United States and its European allies during these talks was to eliminate the recently introduced Soviet SS-20s, each fitted with three warheads capable of hitting major west European targets. Simultaneously with the negotiations Nato planned to deploy, as a counterbalance to the SS-20s, some 464 ground-based cruise missiles and 108 Pershing-2 ballistic missiles. The initial American proposal was the zero-zero option, which involved the United States giving up its plans for future medium-range missiles if the Soviet Union would destroy its existing SS-20s. The Soviet side rejected this but offered to cut SS-20s to match the number of British and French sea- and land-based missiles, allowing for no American medium-range missiles. Other disagreements concerned whether or not SS-20s deployed in Asia or on Asian targets should be counted into the bargaining. There was considerable popular opposition among the European allies of the United States to the deployment of the new intermediate weapons, but in the course of 1983 governments favourable to the Nato plans were returned to power in the United Kingdom, Italy and West Germany. The talks finally broke down with the deployment of the first Pershing-2 missiles in Germany in December 1983.

In the course of the INF negotiations a number of different arms reduction packages were considered, and there were moments when it looked as if some agreement might be in sight. But multilateral negotiations such as Start and INF labour under a number of difficulties inherent in the bargaining process. First, it is difficult for the superpowers to come to agreement about the initial situation. In counting the other side's weapons, each side wishes to "err on the safe side"; and what is the safe side seen from one side of the table is the dangerous side seen from the other. In making comparisons between the two arsenals, each side will favour criteria (number of launchers, number of warheads, throw-weight etc) which will make its own weapons seem more modest and the opponent's more threatening. Secondly, in proposing different formulas for reduction, each side will be more concerned in seeing that it has the better of any bargain than in seeing that any bargain is actually reached. Thirdly, each side will be anxious to go to the negotiating table in the most advantageous position: that is to say, with the greater number of weapons, actual or projected, to be given away as bargaining chips. Procurement decisions of enormous expense are often made on this basis. Entering into multilateral negotiations without bringing them to any successful conclusion has thus become a certain recipe for seeing that the number of weapons deployed, so far from being reduced, actually increases.

One particular defect of the Start and INF negotiations was that they placed nuclear weapons in two separate bargaining contexts in a way which prevented some of the most relevant comparisons from ever being discussed. The United States for instance saw Pershing-2 as clearly an intermediate weapon, capable of use only in the European theatre and therefore tactical. For the Soviet Union, its range brought it far too close to Moscow for it to be considered as anything other than a strategic weapon with dangerous first-strike capabilities. The appropriate comparison was not between Pershing-2s and SS-20s; it was rather with the Soviet submarines, such as the Yankees, which cruise the American coastline with the capability of decapitating the American national command structure in a few minutes.

The Geneva negotiations do not suffer from this defect, since both intermediate and strategic weapons are being discussed under a single overall umbrella. But one error bids fair to be repeated. The Nato plan for the deployment of cruise and Pershing was justified on the grounds that this would make success more likely in the negotiations to remove SS-20s. But the Soviet side was unwilling to trade existing weapons for future ones, and it was the actual arrival of Pershings that caused the talks to fail. Once again, the United States is hoping to use a future system (the "Star Wars" defence in space against ballistic missiles) to bargain away existing weapons already deployed on the other side. The negotiating theory remains that the more threatening the posture of the negotiators the more likely the negotiations are to succeed.

In any rational programme for the elimination of nuclear weapons, multilateral negotiations are going to be essential. But multilateral negotiations will only succeed if they are carried out with a genuine intention of reducing weapons, and not for the purpose of gaining a strategic advantage at a lower level of stockpiling. And they can only succeed if positive steps are made to build up an atmosphere of trust between the participants, which can only be done by unilateral steps to reduce threat and tension.

It is with this practicality in mind that the steps outlined in the previous chapter were selected and placed in order of implementation. But from the moral point of view defended in this book, the renunciation of the actual use of nuclear weapons is in a quite special position.

No First Use

It is placed first not because a public proclamation of the resolve never to use them would be either sensible or credible in isolation from the other steps, but because a genuine policy of renunciation is the essential condition for the rest of the programme being morally acceptable. A declaration that the West will never be the first to use nuclear weapons, parallel to that already made by the Soviet foreign minister, Mr Gromyko, at the second United Nations special session on disarmament, has been repeatedly called for not only by bishops but by former Nato generals and American secretaries of defense. The present Secretary of Defense, Mr Weinberger, has stated that American nuclear weapons will not be used deliberately to destroy populations. If these two declarations were made emphatically, and were rendered credible by the necessary alterations in military planning and targeting policy, we would have moved a long way towards the total renunciation of nuclear weapon use. If neither side uses the weapons first, neither side will use them at all. But of course it is a possibility that the Soviet Union might renege on its pledge of no first use. So a western declaration never to use the weapons first, and never to target them on populations, does not altogether rule out western use: there remains the possibility of retaliatory use on military targets. This too needs to be ruled out, if the military targets are in centres of population. But it is less important to announce such a renunciation than to reflect its genuineness in strategic training and planning.

It is essential, if such a renunciation is to be credible, that it should be accompanied by a freeze on the development of nuclear weapons. The testing, production and deployment of new nuclear weapons should be halted, and so should the planning and building of missiles and aircraft and submarines designed as launching platforms for nuclear warheads. To be effective in stopping the nuclear arms race, a freeze should be a mutual one, observed by both United States and Soviet Union, and every diplomatic effort should be made to that end. But a freeze by the West should not be made conditional upon reduction of Soviet weapons, for that would entangle the proposal in the interminable difficulties of multilateral arms reduction talks.

The proposal for a freeze has many advantages. Of course, by itself it falls well short of even the very modified unilateralism recommended here. But it is an initial goal which anyone who believes in staged disarmament can wholeheartedly support. Naturally, he will support it as an interim measure, not as a finally satisfactory goal. None the less, it has great advantages as a first step towards ending the arms race. Any disarmament goal which is to achieve the massive support necessary to turn it into political reality must be a goal which is easy to grasp and which presents an appearance of being roughly fair between the superpowers. This the freeze proposal does. It has been welcomed by Soviet leaders and endorsed by the United Nations, and it has at times attracted majority support in the American Congress. It has the great merit, if accepted, that it would end attempts by the superpowers to obtain "first-strike" capability which would enable one of them to disarm the other's nuclear capacity by a pre-emptive strike. Most authorities believe that this is an illusory goal, but we know that it has at times been pursued (by the American airforce, for instance, in the time of Secretary McNamara, who resisted the quest), and we know that fear of the other side's achieving it is one of the most potent fuels to the arms race.

A Timetable for Disarmament

Once the production of future nuclear weapons is halted, reduction can begin in the existing armoury. The most recent additions to the intermediate weapons in western Europe are the Pershing-2 ballistic missiles and cruise missiles such as the

Tomahawks installed at Britain's Greenham Common. These were deployed in accordance with the Nato "twin-track" decision of 1979 in the hope that they would either dissuade the Russians from deploying their SS-20 ballistic missiles, or counter-balance these once deployed. The deployment of cruise and Pershing failed completely in the first task: their arrival led to the break-up of the Geneva talks in which they were to have been traded off against the SS-20s, and there are now some 400 of these missiles deployed. They achieve the second task only at the cost of presenting a further strategic threat to the Soviet Union itself; a threat which is seen by the Soviet Union as an attempt to achieve first-strike capability because of the minimal warning time of the Pershing-2s (eight minutes from launch to Moscow) and because of the difficulty of locating and monitoring cruise missiles once dispersed from their bases.

As I have said, the United States was willing to abandon cruise and Pershing if the Russians would dismantle the SS-20s: this was the "zero option". Since 1981 the Soviet Union has been in favour of a different zero option, with no nuclear weapons at all in Europe, whether intermediate range or tactical. General Sir Hugh Beach, the former head of procurement for the British forces, has recently urged that this option should be taken up:

> Up to now the justification for Nato's possession of tactical nuclear weapons in Europe has been threefold: firstly, to deter their use by the Warsaw Pact; secondly, to cramp the style of any Warsaw Pact overland assault by enforcing a high degree of dispersion; and thirdly, to provide an ultimate means of stopping a massive conventional assault. Self-evidently, if both sides dispense with tactical nuclear weapons, the first function is redundant. To the extent that the first function is valid, it makes nonsense of the third; for if the Warsaw Pact is deterred from using their tactical nuclear weapons first by our ability to retaliate, then so are we by theirs. There remains the second, and only strictly military, justification which depends essentially upon the existence of targets which can only be economically attacked by nuclear means. This is the situation today for certain targets in depth, according to military strategists: Warsaw Pact airfields, concentration areas, bridges, bottlenecks and reinforcing

formations. But the technology is now in sight for coping with these targets by non-nuclear munitions.

Voices on the other side of the Atlantic have urged a similar message. In an article in *Newsweek* in December 1983 Mr McNamara put forward an 18-point plan for reducing the danger of nuclear war. Half of the 6,000 nuclear warheads now stockpiled in western Europe should be withdrawn immediately, he said, beginning with obsolete air-defence systems and the atomic demolition munitions intended to block mountain passes on invasion routes. These latter are particularly dangerous, since to be effective they would have to be in place before the war began, and thus their instalment could aggravate the crisis and make war more likely. The remaining nuclear warheads deployed along West Germany's eastern border should be redeployed to rear areas: this would make them less vulnerable to attack and reduce the temptation to use them rather than lose them. A nuclear-free zone of perhaps 60 miles wide should be negotiated with the Soviet Union. The development and deployment of Pershing-2 should be halted unilaterally, since Soviet fears that they may be used for a decapitation strike present a temptation to launch a pre-emptive attack.

McNamara's proposals fall short of Sir Hugh Beach's claim that all nuclear weapons should be withdrawn from the European landmass. But such a withdrawal will even in the most favourable conditions call for a cautious and carefully considered timetable, and it is obviously sensible to begin by withdrawing from the front line those tactical and intermediate weapons which are seen by strategists on both sides as the most dangerous and provocative.

The current Nato strategy with regard to theatre nuclear weapons is indeed difficult to justify, even in military terms. The Supreme Allied Commander in Europe, General Rogers, has said repeatedly that in his opinion any use of nuclear weapons would be virtually certain to escalate to a strategic nuclear war. At the same time, he says that in the event of a Warsaw Pact tank attack, allied defences are so weak that within four or five days he would have to ask the political authorities to release nuclear weapons for use. This is tantamount to saying that our defence of western Europe rests on our willingness to invite a nuclear Armageddon.

General Rogers himself emphasises the risks, in order to urge European nations to invest more heavily in conventional defence. Undoubtedly, a strengthening of conventional defence must accompany any reduction in nuclear weapons. But it is important that conventional defence should not be built up in such a way as to fuel the traditional Russian fears of an invasion from the West, born of their experience in two world wars. It would be rash, for instance, to try to achieve equality or superiority over the Russians in numbers of tanks and other potentially aggressive weapons.

Fortunately, as Sir Hugh Beach says, technical developments hold out a hope of building up a new kind of defence which is effective but entirely non-provocative. The application of microelectronics to armaments makes possible the construction of small precision guided missiles which can seek out and destroy enemy tanks and aircraft and other offensive weapons. Their ability to destroy large and heavily armoured warships was dramatically demonstrated in the Falklands war in 1982. These developments mean that, for instance, an effective defence against a tank can be designed and manufactured at a fraction of the cost of the tank itself.

To work out the detail of an effective and non-provocative conventional defence system for central Europe would call for substantial research. But the main lines of such a strategy have been described by a number of thinkers. A forward defensive zone could be established using the most advanced methods of detecting and disabling invading forces. The armed forces would be equipped with anti-tank, anti-aircraft and anti-ship missiles. Highly mobile squads of troops armed with defensive weapons of high fire power would be deployed against any enemy forces which broke the forward defence zone. Because aircraft are comparatively easy to destroy, but very difficult to identify as hostile or friendly, defence against air attack would not be by interceptor aircraft but by ground-to-air missiles: once hostilities had started, any object detected in the air would be automatically destroyed. The armed forces would have no long-range missiles, tanks or aircraft, nor any warships except fast missile patrol boats for coastal defence.

Recent advances in micro-electronics favour defence of this kind, and are making it increasingly cost-effective in comparison with traditional methods of counter-attack and invasion which are becoming more and more expensive. Tanks, aircraft and warships become more expensive and more rapidly obsolescent in each generation. When the present frigate fleet falls due to be replaced, for instance, it has been estimated that the same real-terms budget that sustained our present fleet of 42 will support just over one and a half vessels. A purely defensive, non-provocative conventional protection for central Europe, by contrast, may well be feasible within existing European defence budgets.

It may be objected that the technological developments which favour the defender against the attacker will be only temporary: Countermeasures will be developed, and history shows that the balance of advantage swings like a pendulum between offence and defence. But this objection forgets that the main purpose of this kind of defence is to prevent the invasion of a country by hostile forces. Without tanks, ships and aircraft, invasion is not possible. For invasion, human beings have to be moved forward across hostile territory. Precision guided missiles may become smaller and smaller, but because human beings remain the same size, means of invasion cannot be reduced in scale and have to be more and more heavily and expensively armoured if they are to protect the human beings inside them.

We are, then, at a particularly favourable moment to replace the theatre nuclear strategy in Europe with a conventional defence which will be effective and non-provocative. The full capabilities of such defence have not yet been explored and tested: but it is an urgent priority that some of the energy and expense which has hitherto gone into the research and development of nuclear weapons and of conventional weapons of an offensive kind should be diverted to the exploration of the possibilities of non-provocative defence. For to the extent that the West's attitude towards the Soviet Union is visibly and unambiguously defensive, the rationale for the Soviet contribution to the arms race is proportionately reduced.

Dismantling Deterrents at Home

Alongside the removal of nuclear weapons from the European landmass the independent deterrents of the minor nuclear powers should be dismantled. If a nuclear freeze had been introduced, the United Kingdom's plans for the proposed Trident force—with a targeting capacity some 14 times that of the present Polaris force—would already have been cancelled. But it can be questioned whether Polaris has, in any case, ever served any useful purpose, even within the logic of deterrence. It is justified as being a weapon of last resort, available to protect supreme national interests in a crisis where American commitment to the United Kingdom might be called into question. The hollowness of this justification has been well exposed by The Rt Hon Enoch Powell, who cannot be accused of a lack of proper concern for British independence. In *The Times* of 1st June 1983 he wrote:

> Suppose that the Soviet Union . . proved so victorious in a war of aggression in Europe as to stand upon the verge of invading these islands—the position, in other words, in which Germany found itself in the summer of 1940. Surely nobody can dispute that that would be for Britain a situation of extreme peril and that a case for our "defence of last resort" would arise if the Russian high command unleashed the equivalent of Hitler's *Operation Sealion*.
>
> Suppose further, because this is necessary to the alleged case for our nuclear weapon as the defence of last resort, that, as in 1940, the United States was standing aloof from the contest but that, in contrast with 1940, Britain and the Warsaw Pact respectively possessed the nuclear weaponry which they do today. Such must surely be the sort of scene in which the Prime Minister is asserting that Britain

would be saved by possession of her present nuclear armament. I can only say: "One must be mad to think it."

Nobody disputes, I believe, that our nuclear weaponry is negligible in comparison with that of Russia: if we could destroy 16 Russian cities she could destroy practically every vestige of life on these islands several times over. For us to use the weapon would therefore be equivalent to more than suicide; it would be genocide.

The actual "supreme national interests" which have been invoked by supporters of the British independent deterrent have been considerably less dramatic than Mr Powell's imaginary scenario. In 1962 I became involved in a press controversy with Mr (now Sir) John Biggs-Davison about the justification of the British deterrent. We needed our own bomb, he said, because we could not expect the United States to risk nuclear annihilation for the sake of Kuwait and Brunei. I inquired whether this meant that Mr Biggs-Davison thought that it was reasonable for a British government to risk annihilation for her interests in Kuwait and Brunei. My question was not answered: but I wonder how many readers can now even remember what were these interests which defenders of the independent deterrent thought should be defended in this suicidal manner.

The dismantling of the British and French independent nuclear systems should assist in securing the withdrawal of Soviet nuclear weapons from European Russia, since it has been a regular plank in the Soviet disarmament platform that British and French warheads should count against Soviet intermediate weapons. Simultaneously, American missiles and bases would be withdrawn from Britain as from the mainland of continental Europe. This is already the policy of the British Labour party, which at its last conference declared: "We are committed to the unconditional removal of all United States nuclear weapons and nuclear bases from British soil and British waters. Labour will therefore take appropriate action to ensure that the United States government removes its nuclear weapons and nuclear delivery systems from British territory."

After the removal of tactical and intermediate weapons, the next task will be the gradual dismantling of the strategic deterrent on each side. The first aim of negotiation should be a reduction in the ratio of nuclear warheads to launching platforms, so as to eliminate systems with multiple independent re-entry vehicles (MIRVs), leaving only single-warhead missiles. MIRVed weapons are the most dangerous of the strategic arsenals. As things are, they invite a first strike against them (since a single warhead hitting them can eliminate multiple warheads) and are themselves adapted to first strike use because of their capacity to make a multiple kill. The remaining long-range missiles should then be eliminated. Several formulas have been suggested to achieve balanced reduction without either side having the right to claim that the other has achieved a preponderance. Agreement on the appropriate formula would be much easier in an atmosphere of improving trust brought about by genuine unilateral steps towards disarmament. In the West, the airborne weapons and intercontinental ballistic missiles (ICBMs) should be reduced until in the final stage before complete elimination of nuclear weapons only the submarine launched ballistic missiles (SLBMs) remained. These are the most difficult to detect and destroy of the existing nuclear arsenal; and if they should become the victims of a perfidious attack collateral damage would be much less than after an attack on land-based systems. The Soviet strategy has not placed the same weight on submarine missile-launchers, and the Yankee submarines and their successors should be eliminated at an early stage of arms reduction since their missiles, like the Pershing-2s, have a very short flight-time which makes them among the most threatening weapons in the existing armouries. Soviet ICBMs in areas away from centres of population would be, like the American SLBMs, the least dangerous forms of weapon and therefore those whose elimination could be reserved for the final stage. If opposed only by the comparatively inaccurate missiles carried by the American submarines, they would themselves acquire a high level of survivability comparable to that of the SLBMs.

The Soviet ICBMs and the American SLBMs would pro

vide, then, a final transitional stage for the existential deterrent to give each side some guarantee against bad faith by the other during the slow stages to the ultimate elimination of nuclear weapons which is already the declared goal of both sides. The objection however will be put to this plan, as it was put to the American Catholic bishops after their pastoral letter, that it is surely wrong and hypocritical to try to extract deterrent mileage from the possession of weapons whose use one condemns absolutely. It is certainly true that it would be hypocritical to acquire nuclear weapons, which one did not intend to use, in order to frighten the other side into disarming. But that is not what is in question: it is a matter of <u>choosing the most prudent and least dangerous method of getting rid of nuclear weapons</u> which we now possess, whether we like it or not, in the face of a dangerous opponent who also possesses them.

Another Way

The position defended in this book differs from that of the American bishops because their defence of the deterrent meant that the servicemen operating the deterrent had to remain willing to use it in action if ordered; and yet this willingness appeared to be condemned by the bishops' condemnation of use. If the proposals made here were adopted, it would become the official policy of the United States and its Nato allies that the nuclear weapons they possessed would never be used: and this would be not simply a declaratory policy but something which was enforced through the procurement policies, military doctrine, logistics, training, operation manuals, war games and manoeuvres. Continuing to maintain the physical operability of the nuclear weapons with the sole purpose of using them as bargaining counters to secure balanced and eventually total reduction of Soviet forces would not involve even a conditional willingness to use the weapons in any warlike role. We said earlier that the maintenance of a power was not, in itself, wrong: it was the maintenance of a power plus a murderous strategy and a willingness to implement that strategy. The transitional

maintenance of the existential deterrent for bargaining purposes need involve no such murderous element.

It may well be true that if the Russians really believed that
the West had been sincerely and permanently converted to a
renunciation of nuclear weapons use, they would feel little
incentive to reduce their own arms below the level at which they
were assured of destroying American society if they chose. If the
SLBMs retain a deterrent value, it is no doubt because the
Russians do not believe in the total sincerity of the policy or fear
that it may be changed by a subsequent administration. But
provided that our resolve is in fact sincere and firm, no stigma
attaches to us if we benefit from Soviet distrust.

No doubt it will call for fine judgment to decide in what state
of readiness the final transitional weapons systems should be
maintained. Too low a state of readiness will diminish their
value as bargaining counters; too high a state of readiness will
call in question the genuineness of our renunciation of their use.
In the case of submarines, for instance, the question will arise:
should they be mothballed, or retained operational and on
station? If they are on station and armed, should their missiles
be targeted, and if so whither? No sensible answer can really be
given to such questions in advance of reaching the stage of
negotiations at which they present themselves. But looking
ahead from the far distance of the present, it seems as if mothballed submarines would be little use for bargaining with a
country which retained ICBMs operational in hardened silos,
whereas submarines armed and targeted as at present would be
incompatible with realistic renunciation of the willingness to
make warlike use of them.

The dismantling of the submarine deterrent was placed last
on the list of the steps to the elimination of nuclear weapons
because of the isolation and invulnerability of SLBMs. But
SLBMs also have the characteristic of being comparatively very
inaccurate: one of the standard objections to the British Polaris
missiles, for instance, is that they are only really fitted for use on
sprawling targets such as centres of population. There is indeed

a paradox in the grading of nuclear weapons: those which are most objectionable in terms of their murderous potential are often those which are least dangerous from the point of view of political strategy and *vice versa*. Thus anti-ballistic missiles, which in themselves satisfy the criteria of just-war making, are politically obnoxious in so far as they violate treaty obligations and present a threat of first-strike capability. SLBMs, on the other hand, though if they were actually used they would most likely be used murderously, are the least dangerous of weapons to retain as bargaining counters, because of their invulnerability and distance from civilian targets.

This paradox is nowhere more visible than in the matter of President Reagan's Strategic Defence Initiative, popularly called "Star Wars". In March 1983 President Reagan announced that he was launching a programme to create a comprehensive space-based anti-missile defence system which would eliminate the threat posed to the civilian populations of the United States and its allies from Soviet strategic nuclear missiles. What plan could be less murderous and more benign that this? The space weapons involved need not even be nuclear weapons. And yet the president's initiative is regarded by many as highly dangerous, and the Russians clearly attach a high priority to keeping the arms race out of space.

As originally announced, the president's initiative was to be an alternative, not an addition, to existing offensive nuclear weapons. As he told a press conference, he wanted some future president, possessed of such a system, to be able to tell the Soviet leader: "I am willing to do away with all my missiles. You do away with yours." The anti-missile defence system was to render nuclear weapons obsolete.

Preliminary studies by physicists and weapons scientists, however, soon reached the conclusion that a complete defence of the general public against Soviet missiles was not practicable. Even had a "leakproof umbrella" against ICBMs been a possibility, this could not defend the American population against cruise missiles launched from submarines off its coast.

Presidential advisers now talk instead of less complex defensive systems, primarily intended to protect military assets. But such systems are obviously seen abroad as measures to heighten American offensive strike capacity, rather than as benign purely defensive measures. Consequently a new, dangerous and expensive spiral may be added to the arms race.

The present book has tried to suggest an alternative system of defence less dangerous and less expensive than Star Wars. In a press conference on the day of the January 1985 Geneva communique, President Reagan defended his initiative thus:

> Isn't it worth researching to see if there isn't some weapon that is more humane and moral than saying that the only defense we have in the nuclear age is that if they kill tens of millions of our people we'll kill tens of millions of theirs?

The president voices eloquently the inhumanity and immorality of our present policies. There must be, as he says, another way.

BIBLIOGRAPHY

The bibliography of nuclear deterrence is immense. I list below only books and articles that I have drawn upon or found particularly helpful.

Anscombe, G.E.M., "Mr Truman's Degree" and "War and Murder" in *Collected Papers,* vol III, Basil Blackwell, 1982

Barnaby, Frank and Windass, S., *What is* Just Defence? *Just Defence,* 1983

Bracken, Paul, *The Command and Control of Nuclear Forces,* Yale University Press, 1983

British Medical Association, *The Medical Effects of Nuclear War: a Report,* Wiley, 1983

Carver, Field-Marshal Lord, *A Policy for Peace,* Faber & Faber, 1982

Chant, Christopher and Hogg, Ian, *The Nuclear War File,* Ebury Press, 1983

Church of England Board for Social Responsibility, *The Church and the Bomb,* Hodder & Stoughton, 1982

Fisher, David, *Morality and the Bomb: An Ethical Assessment of Nuclear Deterrence,* Croom Helm, 1985

Freedman, Lawrence, *The Evolution of Nuclear Strategy,* Macmillan, 1981

Goodwin, Geoffrey (ed.), *Ethics and Nuclear Deterrence,* Croom Helm, 1982

Gray, Colin S., "War-Fighting for Deterrence", *Journal for Strategic Studies,* March, 1984

Kennedy, Edward M. and Hatfield, Mark O., *Freeze!* Bantam Books, 1982

MacLean, Douglas, *The Security Gamble,* Rowman & Allanheld, 1984

McNamara, Robert S., "What the U.S. can do", *Newsweek*, 5th December, 1983

National Conference of Catholic Bishops, *The Challenge of Peace: a Pastoral Letter*, 3rd May, 1983

Neild, Robert, *How to Make up Your Mind About the Bomb*, André Deutsch, 1981

Paskins, Barry and Dockrill, Michael, *The Ethics of War*, Duckworth, 1979

Roberts, Adam and Guelff, Richard, *Documents on the Laws of War*, Oxford University Press, 1982

Tugendhat, E., *Rationalität und Irrationalität der Friedensbewegung und ihrer Gegner*, Europäische Perspektiven GmbH, 1983